THE MYSTERY OF THE HOLY GRAIL
A Modern Path of Initiation

René M. Querido

Rudolf Steiner College Publications

The cover shows a detail from *Parsival Meeting the Fisherking* by David Newbatt (© Wynstones Press, England) 1991.

ISBN: 0-945803-12-5

CONTENTS

Introduction . . . . *iv*

Acknowledgements . . . . *vi*

A Note Concerning Spelling . . . . *viii*

The Significance of the Holy Grail for Our Time 1

The Three Spiritual Streams in Ninth Century Christianity 15

The Quest for the Holy Grail as depicted by Richard Wagner 27

From Joseph of Arimathea to the Arthurian Round 43

Images of Initiation—The Macrocosmic Symbolism of Wolfram von Eschenbach 67

The Eternal Feminine — From Kundry to Sigune 81

The Mystery of the Holy Grail — The Earth as a Living Organism 99

Bibliography 115

INTRODUCTION

In 1947, shortly after I had met Rudolf Steiner's Anthroposophy, friends in Brussels invited me to a performance of Richard Wagner's *Parsifal* at the Royal Opera. The music drama not only made an indelible impression on me, it also stirred many disturbing questions.

Thus my search began, and in a rather short time I had read what ever I could find by Steiner on the subject of the Holy Grail.

Two years later, in 1949, I met Walter Johannes Stein in London, and for the next eight years, until his death in 1957, I heard many lectures by him on this subject. I am especially indebted to him for his patience and warm enthusiasm in taking time to answer the questions of the young, eager, but inexperienced, enquirer that I was.

Years later I began, tentatively at first, to lecture on the subject of the quest for the Holy Grail. I also gave courses on the subject of *Parzival* and the Grail to eleventh grade Waldorf students in Europe and the United States.

Gradually it dawned on me how important this theme is for the development of youngsters around seventeen years old—when they begin to feel poignantly the questions of life and death. Working with boys and girls of this age in different parts of the world helped me to understand the universal relevance of these tales, for they carry a prophetic dimension which makes them as valid now as when they were first composed.

Apart from Rudolf Steiner's indications on the Grail theme, most of which have been translated, there are few commentaries by other authors available in English.

The Mystery of the Holy Grail: A Modern Path of Initiation contains in essence the content of lectures developed over the years particularly in Europe and North America. Though they have been revised for publication, the oral flavor of these lectures has been consciously retained.

It is hoped that this book may fill a gap in the Grail literature available to readers of English. May it quicken and inspire those on the quest to search further and may newcomers to the subject of the Holy Grail be prompted to embark on this wondrous pilgrimage.

R. M. Querido
The Holy Nights
Boulder, Colorado, 1990

ACKNOWLEDGMENTS

I would like to express once again my special indebtedness to Walter Johannes Stein, whose lasting and profound inspiration cannot be valued too highly. Herr Stein, who first taught *Parzival* to the eleventh grade in the original Waldorf School in Stuttgart, was a true Grail teacher.

When Stein sought the advice of Rudolf Steiner as to what he should teach in the eleventh grade, Steiner asked him what he felt especially closely connected with that was appropriate for this age group. Stein replied, "The Grail Sagas." "Well!" responded Steiner, "that would be most suitable."

In the latter part of his life, Dr. Stein became aware of his own deep historical connection with the Grail stream. Though he never referred to this directly in his lectures, many of his listeners felt that they were listening to a man who was speaking out of personal experience. Yet he always was able to lift the material into the clear light of his warm objectivity.

I also wish to acknowledge my gratitude to Steven Roboz of Vancouver, Canada, another student of W. J Stein, for allowing me to include a copy of his bibliographical reference list of Rudolf Steiner's lectures on the theme of the Grail. They can be found in his useful reference booklet entitled *The Holy*

Grail—from The Works of Rudolf Steiner (Steiner Book Centre Inc., Vancouver 1979-1984).

Very special thanks are due to Janet Langley for her tireless efforts in preparing and editing the manuscript for publication.

Finally, appreciation is due to Nancy Whittaker for her careful revision of the text.

A Note Concerning Spelling

The reader will notice throughout this book that the spelling of the names of the principal characters changes, it would seem, almost as many times as they are mentioned. While to modern sensibilities this may appear as a flagrent disregard of basic proof-reading standards, it is actually intentional. During the time in which the Grail legends were a living part of human culture, spelling had not yet been fixed. And so we find Parzival appearing also as Percival and Parsifal depending upon the culture in which the story was told and also, perhaps, upon the ear of the storyteller. We have chosen to retain this quality and hope that our readers find it as invigorating and refreshing as we do.

THE SIGNIFICANCE OF THE GRAIL STORY FOR OUR TIME

For those of you interested in modern spirituality there is perhaps no one theme that is more important than that of the Grail. As early as 1909, Rudolf Steiner (1861-1925) prophetically announced that the Grail stories, with their poignant, poetic quality, depicting the quest towards the highest, would re-emerge in modern consciousness. In fact, modern authors such as T. S. Eliot, Solshenyzin, John Steinbeck, and others have incorporated various aspects of Grail imagery in their writings.

The most important Grail sagas were written around the year 1200 AD. One of the first, *Perceval Le Gallois (Perceval the Welshman)* by Chrétien de Troyes appeared in 1180. Unfortunately, this beautiful poem in Old French was left unfinished. No less than a dozen poets have attempted to bring Chrétien's saga to a fitting conclusion. The second notable Grail work was completed by Wolfram von Eschenbach in 1213. Von Eschenbach relates his *Parzival* in sixteen books or chapters written in Middle High German.

Chrétien's poetic version tells the Grail story from the microcosmic aspect with a minimum of reference to names and heavenly occurrences. Wolfram's conception, on the other hand, is macrocosmic—

fuller and broader, with almost every adventure linked to its corresponding stellar constellation. Both the French and the German versions, however, share the essential elements of a thrilling tale: dramatic battles, intense love themes, tragic sorrow, vivid contrast between good and evil, and the search for the loftiest ideal of mankind. The action unfolds swiftly against a colorful background of castles, forests, lakes, and mountains.

During the Middle Ages, these sagas permeated the lives of the European people. One can imagine how bards and singers would journey from castle to castle. Knowing that they brought lofty entertainment, the local Lord would gladly receive them. After a meal in a great hall illumined with candles, the story teller, imbued with the special festive mood, would sing and recite these Grail sagas. The performers would sometimes remain for a week or more and the nobility would invite the people from surrounding villages to partake of these presentations night after night. As the stories unfolded, people would be deeply touched by the bards' lyrical words. Thus the imaginations and hearts of thousands were transformed by these wandering minstrels.

Although a number of early manuscripts, some beautifully illuminated, are also extant, most of these stories were originally passed on through recitation. Considering them as entertainment might help us in coming closer to their profound character. The English word *entertainment* is related to the French *entretenir*—to maintain, to hold, that which lives between people. These tales were composed by initiates who were able to see more deeply than others into the mysteries of the universe. Their purpose was to present the fruits of their spiritual insights in such a way that in the act of passing them from one human heart to another the truths they contain would find fertile soil and flourish in the community at large. The people of the Middle Ages had a different form of consciousness than we have today, and the truths gained from these stories were experienced through a sense of deep feeling and devotion rather than through rational understanding.

If we look upon these poems as not only great works of art and fascinating legends full of symbolism and historical interest but as a source containing—and Rudolf Steiner paved the way for this understanding—profound occult meaning, their relevance for our own day and age becomes apparent.

Wolfram von Eschenbach said of himself that he could neither read nor write. This admission was an oblique way of saying that he could see into the spiritual world and read the occult script. He further claims that his inspirer was Kyot from Toledo, Spain. During this time (1200 AD), Toledo was, in fact, a remarkable center where students of the Islamic esoteric tradition met with scholars of the Jewish Kabbala and representatives of esoteric Christianity. It is said that for several hundred years Toledo was a place of peace, where the light-filled occult sciences of three principal streams met and fructified one another.

A few hundred years after the above-mentioned French and German sagas appeared, we begin to find various English versions. The most famous was written by Thomas Malory who died in 1471. This epic legend, entitled *Le Morte d'Arthur,* deals essentially with the Arthurian Round, including the origin of the Round Table formed by Merlin the Magician, and the subsequent adventures of King Arthur, Lancelot, Gallahad, and many others. In this particular version Sir Perceval is seen from quite a different perspective and plays a relatively minor part.

Toward the end of the Kali Yuga, or Age of Darkness (3101 BC – 1899 AD), a number of great nineteenth century poets and musicians struggled with the Grail theme of the higher truths. For example, Alfred Lord Tennyson (1809 – 1892), accomplished a tremendous task in his *Idylls of the King,* which brought the stories of the Arthurian Round to the consciousness of his contemporaries. These stories were not only read and appreciated by the Victorian upper class, but to this day play a central part in the education of every boy and girl in England. They spread among the people, conveying a sense of chivalry, honor, and responsibility. Basic virtues were imparted to people as they lived into the sorrowful and joyous adventures of the knights and ladies who quested toward perfection.

The various Grail adventures taken as a whole are imbued with a rare quality. One might say that they were composed in order to awaken the listeners or readers little by little to the loftiest truths. When

Rudolf Steiner speaks in 1909 of how this hidden knowledge will reappear, metamorphosed in a longing for understanding, the modern significance begins to emerge. One can still read and hear these stories with the greatest devotion, but the question now arises, can these sagas become initiation content for us? By delving into the character of Parzival and the sagas surrounding his quest, we may be able to perceive those particular stages along the Grail path that lead the soul to the highest.

The two forms of the name *Parzival* (from the Persian) and *Perceval* (from the French) offer a valuable indication as to the basic character of the hero and the type of ordeals he has to face on his quest. *Parzival* means *pure fool:* one who lives in dullness within his physical surroundings, unrelated to supersensible reality. *Perceval* means *piercing the vale,* and by extension refers to one who goes through the dark valley of death in search of the ultimate light. As we proceed, we shall see that these two *leitmotivs* are basic to a deeper understanding of the story.

The study of these poems reveals certain threads which are common to each saga. Drawing upon both versions freely, we shall follow one of these threads in particular; that is the role of death and its relationship to Parzival's evolution of consciousness.

As the story unfolds, we find Herzeleide, whose name means *heart-sorrow,* in love with Gahmuret, a noble and brave knight. They marry, but Gahmuret is unable to settle down with his beloved and departs on a crusade to the East. After his departure,

Herzeleide discovers she is pregnant and subsequently gives birth to a son named Parzival. When Herzeleide hears that Gahmuret has been slain in battle, she vows to prevent her young son from following in his father's fatal footsteps. Thus she raises Parzival in seclusion, denying him the knowledge of his true name and heritage.

Parzival grows up keenly interested in the physical phenomena that surround him, yet he displays from the outset a dull, insensitive soul life which prevents him from participating in the joy and sorrow of others. His is a spectator's consciousness, severed from all remnants of spiritual participation.

One day, Parzival witnesses a number of knights riding through the forest in their shining armor. In awe of their regal stature, he suddenly develops a burning desire to seek knighthood. True to Parzival's insensitive, thoughtless nature, he makes this decision without understanding the ennobled ideals and life these gallant men represent. Upon hearing his plans, Parzival's mother entreats her son to abandon this impulsive ambition. Failing to dissuade him, Herzeleide attempts to undermine his efforts by dressing Parzival in a jester's costume and then sends him off on an old nag. Impervious to the heart-breaking sorrow he is causing his mother, Parzival rides off into the world without even glancing back. Had he turned around for a final farewell, he would have seen that his mother had fallen down and died of grief.

This marks Parzival's first encounter with death. He is indirectly responsible for his mother's fate and yet is completely unaware of it. In dullness of soul he incurs guilt unknowingly. We shall see that dullness, death and guilt incurred unconsciously color Parzival's subsequent adventures, until an inner awakening occurs.

Shortly after leaving his mother's manor, Parzival enters a richly adorned tent erected in a meadow. There within the tent lies Jeschute, the wife of Orilus, resting alone on a couch. Driven by his thoughtless, awkward nature, Parzival snatches a kiss from the lady's lips. Then he rudely takes her precious jewels and greedily eats of the food Jeschute had prepared for her husband's return. Jeschute is left in a state of complete bewilderment as Parzival leaves her tent, oblivious of the tragic consequences which will follow his foolish deeds.

Orilus, finding his wife Jeschute in a troubled frame of mind, suspects the worst and wrongly accuses her of adultery. Without a moment's delay, he shames his wife by exposing her to public ridicule as an adulteress. He then ventures forth, vowing to take revenge on the evil doer, as soon as he can find him.

On this same afternoon Sigune, Parzival's cousin, and Schionatulander, a knight in service to Parzival's household and Sigune's beloved, are resting in a nearby forest, completely unaware of the above events. Sigune had been reading the cosmic script inscribed in precious stones on the leash of the dog her beloved had caught for her. Suddenly, the dog escapes, dragging the leash behind him. Laughing, Sigune swears that she will not marry Schionatulander until he has caught the dog and allowed her to finish deciphering the heavenly writing on its leash. Concentrating on his pursuit of the dog, Schionatulander is caught off-guard by Orilus, attempts to defend Parzival's lands against the intruder, and is slain. (Other works of Wolfram —eg., *Titurel, Wilhelm,* and *The Story of the Leash* — give additional indications as to the destiny of Schionatulander, including that Orilus mistakes him for the supposedly adulterous Parzival and slays him.)

Let us now attempt to understand the significance of Parzival's second involvement with death. The name Schionatulander is a corruption of the French "chien de la lande," meaning "dog of the heath." Ancient Egyptian mystery knowledge regarded Sirius, the Dog Star, as the heavenly seat of Isis, the source of cosmic wisdom. Therefore, we can surmise that Schionatulander, as his name implies, brought the cosmic wisdom down to the earth so that it might be received by Sigune, the representative of the human soul.

Later in the story, Parzival meets the mourning Sigune who holds her dead lover on her lap in the manner of the *Pieta*. During this meeting, Parzival becomes aware of both the deeper implications of the knight's death and the fact that he himself is partly responsible for this death. Though unable to gain true self-knowledge, Parzival takes a first step toward awakening during this encounter when Sigune reveals to him his real name. She also tells him that he is, unbeknownst to himself, the King of Norgals and that some day he will wear a crown on his head.

She thereby connects him with the intention of his higher being which dwells in the spiritual world. This does not mean that Parzival is as yet able to act in accordance with this newly found knowledge, but that he is given an inkling of the goal he is to attain. However, severe ordeals still await him on his road to the throne of the Grail King.

In the next of these ordeals Parzival's third encounter with death is outwardly a more conscious experience. Through a series of events, Parzival finds himself facing the Red Knight in a jousting match. In normal combat the inexperienced Parzival would not have stood a chance against this brave knight, one of King Arthur's most powerful and noble. Yet, by a stroke of luck, Parzival pierces the Red Knight's visor and kills him. From that point on it is Parzival who is called the Red Knight. Thus through an act of chance, Parzival usurps the great knight's position without going through the required inner discipline and catharsis usually demanded of anyone striving to achieve knighthood. For a true knight consciously stood in the service of spiritual powers, a type of dedication which was to Parzival still incomprehensible.

For Parzival, death still holds no meaning. His actions continue to reveal a profound lack of compassion. There is, however, a marked development, for in this episode of the Red Knight destiny has led him to a death for which he is fully responsible. That he is yet unable to acknowledge this responsibility is due to the dullness that still weighs on him.

It is beyond the scope of this chapter to consider Parzival's many intervening adventures and ordeals. Rather do we intend to pursue the theme of death as the awakener of consciousness, and will, therefore, attempt to show its relevance particularly for our time.

Many of Parzival's adventures are archetypal images *(Urbilder)* of soul experiences that are by no means uncommon today. Dullness of soul, an insensitivity to the death and suffering of others, combined with an unbridled will to action are prevalent in the psyche of modern man.

Rudolf Steiner pointed out that mankind as a whole is crossing the threshold which separates the physical from the spiritual world. If this process takes place unconsciously, in dullness, the danger is that the soul returns lamed or in a state of confusion. The only protection lies in the soul gradually preparing for the experience of the spiritual world through a freely accepted inner discipline of concentration, meditation, etc., as described, for instance, in Rudolf Steiner's book *Knowledge of the Higher Worlds and Its Attainment.*

But to cross the threshold along the path of initiation means to meet death consciously. Every night in sleep we cross the threshold unconsciously. At death, when the physical body is laid aside, the threshold is also crossed, but in such a way that we cannot return to the same body. The initiate, however, is able, as a result of an inner strengthening of his soul powers, to cross the threshold consciously and thus establish continuity between day-waking consciousness and that of sleep.

We now come to the central episode in the story: Parzival's first visit to the Grail Castle. The events described take place in the supersensible, not in the physical world. It is clear that Wagner understood this, for in his sacred music drama, *Parsifal*, Parsifal's teacher leads his pupil into the Grail Castle, and says: *Zum Raum wird hier die Zeit*, "Here time becomes space," indicating a change of consciousness as it occurs in sleep without our awareness, or through initiation consciously.

It was not Parzival's intention to go to the Grail Castle; he was, in fact, led there by his horse. The castle which stands on a mountain is hidden from sight and difficult to reach. Finding himself lost and in need of shelter, Parzival requests and is finally invited by the Fisherman King (Amfortas) to spend the night in the Grail Castle. Once inside Parzival notices that a great sadness weighs on all who dwell in the castle, for Amfortas, the Grail King (his name means *robbed of strength*), is ailing; suspended between life and death, he is no longer able to fulfill his great office and suffers severe pain which nothing so far has been able to remove.

It was known throughout the castle that a "pure fool," if he but freely asked the right question ("Uncle, what ails thee?"), could heal Amfortas. But Parzival, faced with his first major spiritual experience, remains dumb. Although he witnesses the momentous events connected with the Grail ceremony, he is not yet ripe to ask the healing question. The following morning, on awakening,

Parzival finds the Grail Castle empty. Chrétien tells us that by then he would have liked to ask why Amfortas was suffering, but it was to late. Rudely ejected, he finds himself alone and forlorn, on the other side of the moat.

Although this episode is not strictly a meeting with death, it is nevertheless related to it. Parzival crossed the threshold leading into the supersensible world—the world beyond death. But because he was unprepared, he was unable to enter rightly into this realm. As a result, he was rejected, and his former dullness is now replaced by a long period of doubt and suffering. Wolfram tells us that Parzival was involved with evil deeds for the next five years. Though no details are given, we are led to understand that Parzival, estranged from the spiritual world, sinks further and further into the one-sided entanglements of the physical world. For spiritual experiences, if they are not rightly understood, or take place unheeded, can lead to a deeper sinking into matter.

How does Parzival awaken? for it is his destiny to be the future Grail King. Having trodden a long road of suffering that takes him through scorching deserts and icy storms, it is the magic of Good Friday, the death of Christ on the cross, which finally awakens him. For the first time Parzival experiences death consciously and feels Christ's suffering to be his own. His experience of the sacrificial death of the Savior marks the first stage of the healing of Parzival's soul. Once this healing begins, Parzival is ready to receive the Grail teaching from Treverizent, the wise hermit.

Partaking of the Grail, Treverizent tells him, is the basis for true spiritual communion among the living and the dead; yet it also feeds each one according to his own individual need. Here the right Christian harmony is established between the individual and the community, between the self and society. But the process is a gradual one *(Grail—gradalis—gradual)*, leading from dullness through doubt to final spiritual enlightenment—a process where conscious death awakens new life.

It can be said of recent decades that humanity has experienced both an astonishingly rapid progress in the areas of science and technology and an increasingly acute soul-sickness on an individual level. The powers of death are perceptibly tightening their grip. The Grail story can help us to realize that a conscious meeting with death is unavoidable; in fact, it represents the only possible salvation for the soul. Just as the Christ could not have resurrected on Easter Sunday had there been no death on Good Friday, so the modern soul cannot live anew in the spirit, unless it consciously faces the "nothingness," the "abyss" within its own being. Today it cannot be a matter of belief, it must be a question of experience—of treading a path. Parzival's quest for the Holy Grail translates in powerful imaginations the experiences that each modern soul must undergo along a path of inner death and resurrection. Ultimately, it leads the soul to an experience of Christ Himself.

THE THREE STREAMS OF CHRISTIAN SPIRITUALITY IN THE NINTH CENTURY

Wolfram von Eschenbach clearly indicates in *Parzival* that the events he was relating took place historically in the ninth century. This period from 800 to 900 AD marks a significant turning point in the development of Europe and the Middle East: increasing tension occurred between the Christian Holy Roman Empire of Charlemagne, which stood under the sign of the cross, and the expansion of the Arab world led by Haroun al Rashid (786-809) and his successors from Baghdad under the symbol of the crescent moon.

Extending the influence of Mohammedism into the Southwest of Europe were the Moors who invaded France and Spain from North Africa. During the next six centuries their dominance held sway until their final expulsion from Granada in 1492.

The conflicts that began in the ninth century between the Christian and the Moslem world were far-reaching. They can be characterized as the opposition between the Christian people of the Sun, located in Europe, and the followers of Islam under the Moon, who occupied a crescent-shaped territory from the North African western horn which touches the Iberian peninsula, to the eastern horn which points towards Constantinople.

After the middle of the ninth century the conflict took on a more inner character, ultimately shattering the unity of the Christian Church. The Eighth Ecumenical Council of Constantinople concluded its deliberating in 869 AD to discuss, among other topics, the validity of the view that the nature of the human being is threefold, that man consists of body, soul and spirit. At the conclusion of this Council, held in the Hagia Sophia (Place of the Divine Wisdom), it was decreed that the human being consisted only of body and soul (with the soul bearing certain characteristics of the spirit). This decree had far-reaching repercussions for the future of humanity. For this abolition of the spirit (this is the actual phrase that was used in the decree, "to *abolish* the spirit") resulted in the denial of both the independent "I am" of the human being and its unique nature capable of re-embodiment. A tragic dualistic view of humanity ensued which proved fatal for the true understanding of both death and the after-life.

A thousand years later the essence of man was even further negated by modern psychologists, such as Freud, who virtually proclaimed that the source of all soul manifestations could be traced back to bodily functions. This view was enhanced by such influential thinkers as Marx and Engels who further contributed to the materialistic image of man that is still so prevalent today. Therefore, with the Church having abolished the spirit and science having rejected the existence of the soul, modern man is considered as being little more than the product of purely physical forces.

The Council of 869 had other repercussions as well. It was so controversial that it caused the Church to split into three separate streams of Christian spirituality. In a somewhat simplified form the situation can be summarized as follows: The Roman Catholic Church recognized the abolition of the spirit and intensified its reliance on faith and dogma. The deeper mysteries of the Christ Spirit, it was felt, could never be the object of experience on the part of the laity. Therefore, the devotees of this path were taught that only a true feeling for and belief in the Church could lead to salvation. This reliance on Church dogma and faith had, in fact, already been initiated by Pope Nicholas I who died in 867, two years before the decree of Constantinople was finally issued. Though it was Nicholas' intent to maintain the validity of the Church as founded by Peter, records show that it was unlikely that he would have been in favor of a final abolition of the spirit.

Unable to support the direction the Roman Church was taking during the ninth century, the Russian Orthodox movement established its own Church. While it maintained the threefold nature of man as self-evident, the Russian Orthodox Church put forth no dogma and was essentially concerned with the mystic significance of the ritual, which in word and music inspired the congregation to the deepest soul experience of oneness with the Christ. Communion united individuals in worship so that their lives on earth might become more meaningful. This represented a path of the will, in which ritual stood foremost and was celebrated in churches richly decorated in gold and icons, where their sublime sanctity was enveloped in the beauty of word and sound.

The third stream, the Grail Stream, emerged mainly in the West. It was comprised of those "heretics and false believers" who continued to maintain the reality of the threefold nature of man as body, soul and spirit. The Grail Stream divided into two parts, the more Celtic Arthurian Stream and the Grail Stream represented by Parzival. The Grail impulse would later extend to include the Cathars, the Bogoumiles, and the Waldensians.

The Arthurian Grail Stream, which shunned the dogmatic belief in Church forms that could not be understood, was also unwilling to embrace the mystical ritualistic path as practiced by the Eastern Churches. Instead it united with esoteric Irish Christianity and sought a path of gradual inner development through individual meditation, catharsis, and enlightenment—a path which would lead to an understanding of the profoundest mysteries surrounding the Being of Christ.

Karmically, we can see how our own age is connected with these events of the ninth century, especially with the Council of Constantinople. More than a thousand years have passed since the spirit was denied; more recently mankind has lost sight of his soul, plunging him into the darkness of believing that only the body, the material part of his being, has reality. Therefore, unless we come to a clear and living understanding of the spirit, the lawful working of reincarnation can have little meaning for the

The Three Streams of Spirituality in the Ninth Century

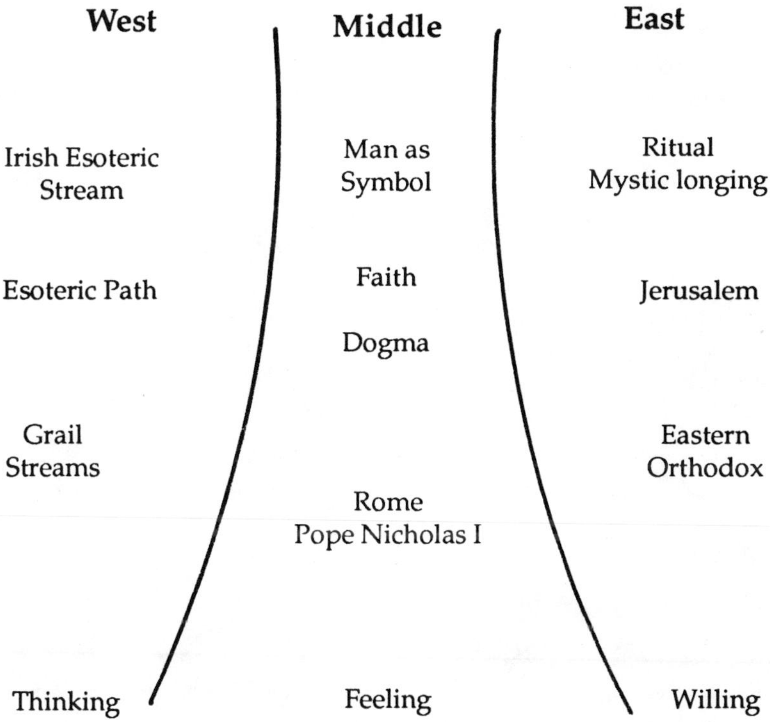

This separation occurred as a result of the Council of Constantinople's 869 AD decree "abolishing the Spirit."

western mind. Toward this end Rudolf Steiner's first step when renewing the Grail Mysteries at the beginning of the Age of Light in 1899 was to re-establish the trichotomy of man's being as consisting of body, soul and spirit.

The spirit, the unique self, the essential "I am" of every human being, is that which is eternal in each individual. Governed by the laws of reincarnation, the spirit is present before each birth and survives beyond each death. During life the spirit shines through our biography as the Higher Self. Our body, formed out of the elements of the earth, offers an abode, a temple for our spirit. Unlike the spirit, the body's very nature is transient, subject to birth and death, "ashes to ashes, dust to dust."

The soul can be viewed as the mediator between the eternal self and the transient body, relating to both spirit and matter. Between death and rebirth the spirit weaves its next life's destiny into the soul, and as the seat of our destiny it is therefore influenced by both the eternal "I am" in each one of us and that which arises from our bodily constitution. The soul is the inner stage upon which the development of man is enacted. For instance, the experiences and happenings of the day are digested by the soul. But wishes, intentions, and those ideals which have their source in the spirit also pass through the soul before they lead to action. The soul responds, on the one hand, to outer stimuli; on the other, it is receptive to the inner inspiration of the spirit. Body and spirit meet in the soul, which is the bearer of our destiny.

This trichotomy of the human being is

characterized with fundamental simplicity in Rudolf Steiner's book *Theosophy* (1904) which, one might say, represents the first complete refutation of the Council of 869 AD. (It should be pointed out that *theosophy* means *wisdom of God*. It can also be interpreted that the human being is the wisdom of God, for truly man is the crowning work of art of the gods. Hence, we find that Steiner's book presents the nature of the human being as the creation of the Godhead.)

> Man looks up to the heavens: the joy which he experiences in his soul is his own; the eternal laws of the stars, which he encompasses in his spirit by means of thinking, are not his own, they belong to the stars themselves.
>
> Thus man is a citizen of three worlds. Because of his body he belongs to this world, which he also experiences by means of his body; by virtue of his soul he elaborates his own world; by means of his spirit a world reveals itself to him which goes beyond both.

Rudolf Steiner proclaimed that only through conscious spiritual development will the reality of man's threefold nature be rediscovered. Seen in this light, the quest for the Holy Grail reflects in imaginative form the modern search for man's true being through stages of dullness and doubt to final spiritual awakening.

The perfect representative of this path is, of course, Parzival, who grows from dullness to doubt to achieve ultimate initiation as King of the Grail, in

Saelde, a *blessed* inner condition out of which he can serve others.

Wagner characterized this from yet another aspect when he tells us that Parsifal treads the path "durch Mitleid wissend," "through compassion to knowing," to a personal, individual experience of the highest: the Grail itself. This is not based on dogma, faith or ritual, but on the conscious transformation of our soul forces, so that a communion in knowledge with the living spirit might be achieved.

In this context let us consider a passage from Steiner's *Occult Science.*

> We read of the Holy Grail in old-times narratives and legends, and as we learn to understand its deeper meaning we discover that it most significantly pictures the heart and essence of the new Initiation-knowledge, centering in the Mystery of Christ. The Initiates of the new age may therefore be described as the "Initiates of the Grail." The pathway into spiritual worlds . . . culminates in the Science of the Grail.

To help fathom the deepest significance of the various Grail sagas, it is necessary to distinguish the different levels of understanding within the stories themselves. The following is a "Seven-Step Ladder of Understanding" which describes different ways one might study or experience a Grail story.

The seven steps begin at the bottom with the simplest form of understanding (the plot) and move upward in complexity and increased significance until the esoteric level is reached.

THE SEVEN LEVELS OF UNDERSTANDING OF THE GRAIL STORIES

Step 7	The esoteric level: The quest for the Grail as a path of initiation
Step 6	The symbolic significance
Step 5	The historical background: the time of Christ the ninth century the thirteenth century
Step 4	The portrayal of individualities in the course of successive incarnations
Step 3	The psychological significance (the interplay of the characters)
Step 2	The poetry—the language—the form
Step 1	The plot—the action—the story

To understand further how these levels might be employed when reading the Grail sagas, I have elaborated each step as follows:

Step 1. All of the Grail stories have one thing in common: they are told in a remarkably fine way. The plot, the action, the storyline, the content comprise the aspects of the first level and can be appreciated by anyone. (The very fact that Wolfram von Eschenbach's *Parzival* has been available in several paperback editions in the United States, as well as numerous other translations in French and modern German, testifies to its current popularity.)

Step 2. The original works of Wolfram von Eschenbach and Chrétien de Troyes were composed in Middle High German and Old French, respectively. These versions are regarded in scholarly circles as examples of the exquisite poetry of the Middle Ages; even in translation one can admire the use of the language and the style of these two medieval poets.

Step 3. The third level points to the psychological significance, the sensitive ways in which the interplay of the characters are portrayed. Both Chrétien de Troyes and Wolfram von Eschenbach had a subtle understanding of the workings of the human soul.

Step 4. The fourth level pertains to the portrayal of the individualities in the course of successive incarnations. Kundry is a case in point, and Wagner intuitively places her former incarnation as Herodias at the time of the Mystery of Golgotha. Parsifal's previous embodiment can also be traced back to that time.

Step 5. Then there are the historical aspects. Wolfram tells us in his *Parzival* that the story he is relating took place eleven generations before his time, which would date it around the middle of the ninth century (allowing 33 years per generation). As discussed earlier, this was around the time of the Council of 869 AD, when the threefold nature of the human being was rejected by the Church.

Step 6. The sixth level involves reflection on the story's symbolism. Clothed in the imagery of the

Middle Ages, every event carries with it a particular symbolic significance: the spear, the chalice, the fool's clothing, the Red Knight, the sword of Amfortas. These images represent a great deal more than just their physical counterparts.

Step 7. The seventh and highest level represents esoteric understanding—the quest for the Holy Grail as a path of initiation. Sleep, death and initiation are interrelated experiences. Every night, upon falling asleep, we cross the threshold into the spiritual world and return in the morning with little awareness of our experiences when we were out of our body. At the time of death, this same landscape opens further, though there is no longer any possibility of returning to the same body.

The initiate is one who gradually awakens while asleep. Angelus Silesius, the German mystic (1624-1677), referred to this when he said, *Unless you die before you die, you perish when you die.* The initiate has crossed the threshold consciously into the realm of death and then brought back these experiences to his daily life in full consciousness.

The visit to the Grail Castle, where Parzival spends the night, can be looked upon as a dream sequence. So, too, can the sojourn of Gawain into the Castle of Wonders where he endures many ordeals. The very word *Grail* comes from *gradalis*—step-by-step, gradually. Each of the Grail stories speaks of the various individuals' step-by-step development. It is only through catharsis, a transformation of the lower self, that they attain the highest.

In the beginning, Wolfram von Eschenbach describes Parzival as being foolish and dull—so dull that he shows no interest in the human beings around him. Through a number of painful ordeals, Parzival's dullness gives way first to doubt and vacillation and then to the painful struggle as he searches for truth. Finally, he awakens to his true task and realizes the harm he has done to others. Wishing to compensate, to atone for his deeds, Parzival rises to an inner condition of soul-fullness, where he is able to bestow love and healing on his fellow human beings. Wolfram characterizes this condition as *Saelde* which contains the word *Seele,* meaning *soul.* An equivalent of *Saelde* might be termed *blessedness,* though it should be understood as an active condition of giving, of bestowing upon the world.

It is possible to use this heritage, which we have received from the Grail legends over the past seven hundred years, as a path of inner development. By meditating on a particular theme or character (eg., Sigune with her dead lover on her lap, the theme of death, or perhaps the destiny of Parzival or Kundry) and following this chosen stream through the seven levels of understanding, it is possible to elevate one's consciousness from the physical (death) through the intellectual (doubt) to the spiritual.

I would like to close with a verse by Rudolf Steiner (translated by Arvia MacKaye Ege). Though it was originally composed in response to Hölderlin's "Song of Destiny," I think it embodies the striving quality of the search for the Holy Grail.

To us it is given at no stage ever to rest.
They live and they strive the active
Human beings from life unto life.
As plants grow from springtime
To springtime—ever aloft,
Through error upward to truth,
Through fetters upward to freedom,
Through illness and death
Upward to beauty, to health and to life.

Uns ist gegeben,
Auf keiner Stufe zu rasten.
Es leben, es streben die tätigen
Menschen von Leben zu Leben
Wie Pflanzen von Frühling zu Frühling
Sich steigernd durch Irrtum
Zur Wahrheit hinauf,
Durch Fesseln zur Freiheit hinauf,
Durch Krankheit und Tod
Zu Schönheit, Gesundheit and Leben hinauf.

THE QUEST FOR THE HOLY GRAIL AS DEPICTED BY RICHARD WAGNER

The year 1879 marks a turning point in connection with the dissemination of the Grail stories. Many are no doubt familiar with the fact that Rudolf Steiner speaks of this year as the beginning of the Age of the Archangel Michael, a Sun Being. As Rudolf Steiner pointed out repeatedly, Michael is only interested in the essential human being and has no regard for the differences in race, nationality or creed. He appeals solely to the eternal "I am" that lives in every soul.

Now, it is symptomatic that Richard Wagner (1813-1883) completed his sublime music drama, *Parsifal,* during 1879. This last of Wagner's music dramas, and perhaps the most profound, was performed for the first time in 1882, shortly before the composer's death. Wagner was not only a musician and a poet, he was also champion of the idea of the *Gesamtkunstwerk:* the total work of art. This concept of uniting the arts was an ideal to which he devoted an enormous amount of time and energy. The Festspielhaus at Bayreuth was the first implementation of his persistent striving. Here, for the first time in the development of modern humanity, a building was erected which merged together architecture, sculpture and painting in order to create a worthy space in which music, poetry, drama, and movement could come to their full expression.

The uniting of the arts plays an essential role on the path of initiation. That the arts were once the handmaidens of religion can be seen clearly in all ancient civilizations. It was through architecture, sculpture, painting, music, drama, poetry and movement that the souls of ancient times were able to find healing and acceed to the highest.

One could elaborate that each of the classical art forms expresses a different aspect of the human being. For instance, architecture is intimately related to the physical body, sculpture to the formative forces, painting to the emotional life, etc. For a modern path of initiation to be wholesome and harmonious, the unity of all the arts must be gradually focused within the striving human being. In 1907, during a festival gathering in Munich, Rudolf Steiner stated that in the future it will be necessary that the arts and paths of inner development shall never again be severed.

This unification was accomplished in seed form by Richard Wagner in 1879. He initiated the sacred music drama which combines all the arts as a totality and thereby bestows a renewing impulse upon the quest for the spiritual world. If this ideal is understood in its wider implications, one can easily see why Wagner did not want his ritualistic festive music dramas performed anywhere else but in Bayreuth. He felt that without a worthy physical space the true mystery intent of his mighty compositions could not come to expression.

Wagner's prolific musical outpouring culminated in the sublime Christ-centered music drama *Parsifal.* Although he had little regard for conventional denominational Christianity, Wagner had tackled Christian themes in his operas *Tannhäuser* and *Lohengrin* with a considerable measure of success. Yet nothing can be compared with the depth of expression that we find in *Parsifal,* a great mythological drama depicting atonement and redemption.

The original inspiration for this great drama can be traced back to a specific spiritual experience of Wagner's. In the early phase of his life, Wagner experienced a number of serious crises. For years he was a refugee, not only because of his revolutionary political views but also because he was pursued by his many creditors from country to country. It was during his early forties that he found a period of respite owing to his friends, the Wesendoncks, who offered him a small villa on the slope of a mountain overlooking the Lake of Zurich in Switzerland.

Wagner recounts how one morning in spring, as he stepped out of the French windows to admire the rising sun, he had an overwhelming experience which filled his soul with awe and devotion. Gradually the rays of the rising sun pierced through the mists that hovered and shrouded the lake below. This pageant of light continued until the blue waters and the green meadows of the slope became visible, as if celebrating a resurrection in nature. He felt the profound uniqueness of the moment and wondered what was so special about this particular day that it should be heralded by such a sublime dawn. Turning back into the villa and consulting a calendar, Wagner found to his amazement that it was Good Friday, the day commemorating the crucifixion of Christ Jesus, when the blood of the Redeemer on the cross was collected by Joseph of Arimathea in the Grail chalice. Wagner felt this soul-shattering experience both visually and musically, for it was at this time that he heard the opening chords of what was to become the *Karfreitagszauber*-music, the theme of Good Friday. Many years later, this music would become one of the central themes in *Parsifal*.

Wagner had this profound Christ experience not through worship in a church or through human intercourse, but in beholding the magical resurrection forces in nature herself. We could characterize it as Celtic in nature: the search for the divine in the surrounding living garment of the earth. This spiritual theme frequently occupied Wagner over the next twenty years.

When Wagner was sixty-four years old, he began to work on a music drama based on the story of Parsifal. Though he studied various Grail sagas, Wagner's *Parsifal* reflected his own personal insight and experiences. After dedicating himself to this theme for three years, Wagner completed *Parsifal* in 1879.

Rudolf Steiner, during the early years of his life, was by no means a "Wagnerian." It was only in his forties that Steiner gradually found a relationship to Wagner's music. He then began to speak of him quite frequently. In one lecture Steiner reveals that the music of Wagner's *Parsifal* prepares the life forces in every human being who hears it to receive the Christ This occurs, he said, whether the listener is aware of it or not, for the music has a special magic quality. Since its first performance in 1882, hundreds of thousands of souls have been prepared to receive the substance of the Christ through the music and the words of this most inspiring composition.

The fact that Wagner's *Parsifal* is increasingly performed for thousands of souls all over the world reveals that there is a subtle, yet growing interest in the Grail theme which is shared by people in cultures as diverse as those of Europe, North and South America, Japan, and Australia. This is just another indication of the universality of Wagner's *Parsifal*.

It is interesting to note that Wagner does much more than just borrow themes from the stories as given by Chrétien de Troyes and Wolfram von Eschenbach. In fact, Wagner literally reforges the material and creates a totally new drama in three acts. Wagner always found his inspiration in the living word. He accomplished this by allowing the music to flow out of the poetic form itself.

Let us now consider Wagner's *Parsifal* more closely. The opening scene of the music drama finds Gurnemanz, Parsifal's teacher, in a deep forest in the Grail's domain. (It should be noted that Wagner's Gurnemanz is more akin to Trevrizent, the good teacher in Wolfram von Eschenbach's version, and has no relation to Wolfram's character of Gurnemanz who advises Parzival not to ask too many questions!) As the first scene unfolds, we see that Gurnemanz is troubled by his inability to find a cure that would heal Amfortas' wound. Both Gawain and Kundry have attempted to bring him relief and have failed. Gurnemanz commiserates, wishing that the healer would come—the one whom Amfortas describes as "by pity wakened, the blameless fool." This "fool" refers to Parsifal.

As he reflects on Amfortas' words, Gurnemanz realizes that the wounded King's savior will have to retrieve the "wondrous, wonder-working, holy spear" which holds the magic to heal the old Grail King. The spear, however, is in the possession of Klingsor, the black magician, who dwells in his dark magic realm in the desert. Gurnemanz tells us that wresting the spear from Klingsor will not be an easy task:

> Wondrous gardens he created,
> where maids of charms unholy flower
> there for the Grail's pure knighthood
> hath waited to snare by lust and magic's power
> whom once he lures, never frees he any;
> already hath he ruined many.

Shortly thereafter, Parsifal shoots a swan in flight and a young squire sings of the dying wild swan as it falls to the earth. Parsifal then encounters Gurnemanz who immediately begins to ask him questions, including who he is and what he is doing there. To each question Parsifal responds, "That I know not." Exasperated by this useless litany, Gurnemanz sings, "So dull a one I never found save Kundry here."

Upon further reflection, Parsifal does remember that he has a mother named Herzeleide *(Heart-in-sorrow)*. Upon hearing the newcomer speak his mother's name, Kundry reveals to Parsifal the sad news that his mother has died of grief. Parsifal also learns of the pain that Amfortas has been suffering, and asks the strange question, "Who is the Grail?"

At this point we move from the outer forest to the inner space of the Grail Temple. Wagner achieved this transformation by means of a revolving stage where the trees of the forest were designed to become the columns of the Temple. Words of the greatest significance are sung, as both Parsifal and Gurnemanz disappear from sight through a gateway in the side of a rocky precipice. Their path appears to ascend through walls of rock, until the scene has, by degree, entirely changed. The two are then seen entering the mighty hall of the Grail Castle. Gurnemanz says, "Thou seest, my son, to space time changes here." *(Du siehst, mein Sohn, zum Raum wird hier die Zeit.)* Time becomes space.

This transformation of time into space is, in fact, what happens when we cross the threshold from the sense-perceptible to the supersensible world each night when we go to sleep. We can sometimes experience this "space-time" change, as we drift in and out of sleep, when a panorama which seems to span many hours unfolds in a matter of minutes. In recent years, it has also become common knowledge that a person who is close to death from drowning or some other accident sees his life in a split second as a gigantic expanding panorama in which all of his life experiences appear as if in space. The time sequence, the chronology of events, is no longer present.

Similarly, Wagner points out intuitively that the experiences in the Grail Castle—though certainly enacted on the earth itself—are of a supersensible nature, which can be likened to a dream sequence. It is at this time that the sacred Grail celebration is enacted and Parsifal witnesses Amfortas' pain. He still fails to awaken to his task and ask the question. The first act closes as Gurnemanz chides Parsifal:

> Thou art nothing but a fool!
> In future leave our swans alone,
> Thou art but a goose.

Before considering the second act, which takes place in Klingsor's enchanted castle and gardens, let us look at the fascinating character of Kundry, who is torn between her longing to serve the Grail and the curse that binds her to Klingsor's forces of black magic. In the beginning of the first act, when we meet Kundry, she is referred to as a heathen and a sorceress. Confirming this, Gurnemanz tells us that she is living under an ancient curse. He reveals that in a previous life, Kundry was Herodias, the wife of Herod Antipas and mother to Salome. Thus, with astonishing intuition, corroborated by Rudolf Steiner, Wagner relates Kundry to the events at the time of Christ.

Here, we will briefly describe the events of the story of Herodias from the New Testament. Herod Antipas had arrested and imprisoned John the

Baptist for lashing out against the immorality of his family. Concurrently a festival was being celebrated featuring the dancing of Herodias' daughter, Salome. Herod was so entranced by Salome's alluring dance of the seven veils that in a moment of ecstasy in front of his entire court he offered to grant her anything her heart desired. Unsure of what to ask for, Salome consulted her mother, who urged her to ask for John the Baptist's head to be delivered to her on a silver platter. Herod, for fear of losing face, acquiesced and had the holy man beheaded.

The bleeding head of John the Baptist on the silver platter has often been referred to as an image of the Anti-Grail. Obviously Herodias' vicious request intimately connects her with this black magic stream. In a painful, dramatic way Herodias also made a connection with Christ Jesus. Legend tells us that Herodias was standing in the crowd on the Via Dolorosa when Christ was carrying the cross. As He passed by her, Herodias could see that His countenance was filled with perspiration and blood which streamed down from the crown of thorns He bore on his head. Instead of feeling compassion in her heart for His suffering, she scorned Him and spat in His face.

The cold, heartless feelings displayed by Herodias stand in stark contrast to the love and compassion exhibited by another woman in the crowd whose name was Veronica. As Christ passed in front of her, Veronica placed her handkerchief on His suffering face, hoping to alleviate some of His pain. Subsequently we shall see that Veronica plays an essential part in the unfolding of the Grail story, as does Herodias, who becomes Kundry.

When Rudolf Steiner was asked what the essential nature of his own task was, he replied that it was the practical teaching of karma and reincarnation. This one example of the relationship between Kundry and Herodias opens up new vistas of understanding. It places the characters in the Grail stories during their former embodiment around the time of the Christ Mystery. Rudolf Steiner confirmed that Wagner was correct concerning Kundry's incarnation in the Holy Land and stated that another character central to the Grail story was also incarnated at the time of Christ.

The second act takes place in and around Klingsor's enchanted castle. Wagner expressed clearly that during the whole of the second act in the Castel Merveil, the Castle of Wonders, the gardens and costumes were to be set in an Arabian style. As the act begins, we find that six flower maidens, together with Kundry, have been instructed by Klingsor to seduce Parsifal and thus prevent him from following his path toward becoming the Grail King. A similar fate had befallen Amfortas, who had been seduced and then seriously wounded in his sexual organs; a wound which prevented him from standing, sitting or even lying down. Such a fate did Klingsor have in store for Parsifal.

The task of luring Parsifal away from his preordained path ultimately fell to Kundry. Klingsor calls to her:

> Hell's rose blossom! Witch primeval!
> Herodias thou wert.

Come here, come hither Kundry,
thy master calls: obey!

Slave to the black curse she is under, Kundry reluctantly agrees to tempt Parsifal, whom she recognizes as the pure fool. The maidens dance and sing alluringly, while Kundry attempts to seduce him. She then tells Parsifal his true name and how his mother, Herzeleide, died of a broken heart. Just as he is about to succumb to Kundry's wiles, Parsifal experiences in his heart, one might say in his feeling life, the intense pain of Amfortas' spear wound. Amfortas' agony becomes his own, and he cries out, "Amfortas, the spear wound, the spear wound in my heart; it is burning!"

This, indeed, marks a turning point, for it is the first time that Parsifal feels the suffering of another as his own. What he lacked above all was compassion for others—*Mitleid* (from the German, *mit* or *with* and *Leid* or *suffering*)—to *suffer with* the other person. For Wagner this moment represented a crucial awakening when Parsifal gains insight through compassion, *durch Mitleid wissend.* As we saw earlier in the story, it was this lack of compassion, this lack of fellow feeling that prevented Parsifal, when he was in the Grail Castle witnessing the suffering of Amfortas, from asking the question that would have healed the Fisherman King.

Parsifal now tells Kundry that he will be able to redeem her. Klingsor, in a desperate attempt to wound and destroy him, hurls the "wondrous" spear at Parsifal. With extraordinary presence of mind,

Parsifal manages to seize it in mid-air and holds it over his head. He then swings the spear in the sign of the cross and sings, "Now, now with this sign destroyed be thy magic." The Castle immediately collapses, as by an earthquake; the garden withers to a desert and the ground is covered with faded flowers. Thus the Castle of Wonders, the Castel Merveil of Klingsor, is annihilated through Parsifal's deed. The white magic of the Grail has triumphed over black magic. It is then announced that a new king will, as a trustee, be named regent to the Round Table.

As the third act begins, we find that the white magic of the Grail has already touched many of the characters' lives. Kundry sings of her desire to serve, and Parsifal gains an ever-increasing knowledge of himself. At this time, Gurnemanz helps Parsifal to realize how many of his past deeds had brought sorrow and pain to others. The suffering Parsifal experiences for each of his "victims" leads him to an inner transformation. It is after this that he learns he has been chosen to become the Grail King.

As the priest king, the first office Parsifal performs is to baptize Kundry. Then he beseeches her to trust in the Redeemer. Upon hearing these words, Kundry sinks to the ground and weeps passionately. Thereupon Parsifal sings, "How fair me seems the meadowland today." Gurnemanz responds telling him that this is the magic spell of Good Friday which has now begun to work, *"Das ist Karfreitagszauber."* We are reminded here, as the culmination of the opera draws near, of the original inspiration that moved Wagner so deeply—that inspiration which occupied him off and on for twenty years, until it found its completion in this most sacred of music dramas, *Parsifal*.

The ending of the opera is one of rare solemnity: two processions of knights enter the Grail Castle, whereupon Amfortas is healed by a touch of the "wondrous" spear that Parsifal had retrieved from the evil hand of Klingsor. In a most festive and solemn culmination, Parsifal sings of the Holy Spear which had pierced the side of Christ and has now been restored to the Grail Knights. The music drama closes with a mighty chorus singing of salvation and redemption.

Let us leave our retelling of *Parsifal* with a quote from Wagner describing how he intended for this scene to be played.

> The ray of light falls from above and the Grail glows brightest. From the dome descends a white dove which hovers over Parsifal's head. Kundry, with her gaze uplifted towards Parsifal, sinks slowly, lifeless to the ground. Amfortas and Gurnemanz kneel in homage before the new Grail King, who lifts the Grail in blessing over the worshipping knighthood.*

In closing, a few points still need to be made. As we enter more deeply into the various sagas, the question arises, what is the quest for the Holy Grail and what is the nature of the Holy Grail? It appears, at first sight, to be a quest for the chalice that contains the blood of Christ. But, symbolically, esoterically, it represents much more than just a search for a physical chalice or vessel containing the blood of Christ. Rather the Quest represents the striving of the individual to obtain the highest, the purest truth and goodness within himself.

The blood of Christ, which was held in the Grail, also has a deeper esoteric significance. Christ's blood did not contain the hereditary forces of Adam and Eve which were tainted by the Fall precipitated by Lucifer and by all that has followed in the course of human evolution. It was instead purified, sacrificial, untainted. To succeed in the Quest for the Holy Grail would result in the freeing of one's being from the shackles of past deeds; transforming inner darkness to radiant light through a conscious striving to attain the highest ideals.

In interpretations of esoteric material, we face a particular problem today. Understanding the deeper significance of legends was easier when mankind recognized them as having a spiritual reality and acknowledged them as having occurred on earth. Since the dawn of the new Age of Light in 1899 AD, it has become ever more important to unite the esoteric and exoteric aspects of knowledge and experience. This quest challenges us to discover that the inner and the outer are but one, and yet calls upon us to distinguish the two levels clearly.

This challenge was posed by Rudolf Steiner in the very title of a book that he published in 1900, entitled *Christianity as Mystical Fact—Das Christentum als mystische Tatsache.* A little later, Rudolf Steiner coined the expression "the Mystery of Golgotha" as a term encompassing all of the events surrounding the Christ impulse. Were these events facts or were they only mystical experiences? They were and are both of these things, Steiner tells us, factual and mystical at the same time. As we shall see later, there are a number of legends that speak of the origin of the cup or vessel that was used by Joseph of Arimathea to collect the blood of Christ. Both the vessel and the blood belong to the deepest symbols of esoteric Christianity. For the "holy thing" and the "sacred blood" represented, throughout history, the healing and nourishing influences to which human beings could accede. It is said, for instance, that the content of the Grail Cup, if placed at the center of a community that has rightly come together in His name, can nourish each in accordance to his/her own needs.

However, in Wagner's version the question is put differently, for Parsifal asks innocently, and it appears to be a sign of his dullness, "*Who* is the Grail?" not "*What* is the Grail?" At a deeper level, this question is not as foolish as it might appear. In early Christian writings before the fifth century, we find an answer in a sermon by St. John Chrysostomos. He describes the Jesus Child as being like a crescent moon who received the Sun when he grew up and was baptized at the age of thirty. It was only for a period of less than three years that the divine Christ Being dwelt within the body of Jesus of Nazareth. It was as if the moon-like temple of the body of Jesus received the divine content of the Sun Being. The Grail Cup was likened to the body or the temple and the blood contained in it to the spirit "I am" substance that fills the vessel. Reflecting upon this imagination, we might find that Parsifal's question, "Who is the Grail?" is not as foolish as it first appears. For Christ Jesus made manifest the Grail on earth through His body and His blood from the baptism in the Jordan until the crucifixion.

* Touched by the solemnity of this most remarkable music drama, one can well imagine why Wagner was so insistent that *Parsifal,* the last work he was to create, should only be performed in Bayreuth. A month or so before his death on February 17, 1883, Wagner wrote a final letter to King Ludwig II, his faithful friend who had funded many of his productions and had provided the means whereby the Bayreuth Festival Hall could be built. This letter, dated January 10, 1883, attempted one last time to convince the King to prevent the opera from being performed elsewhere. In one respect we can be grateful that he did not succeed, for relatively few people would have been able to experience the drama's magic which reveals the Christ weaving in the mantle of the earth. And yet, one can also appreciate Wagner's desire to have it performed only in a worthy setting.

FROM JOSEPH OF ARIMATHEA TO THE ARTHURIAN ROUND

Let us begin today with a quotation from Chapter Six of *An Outline of Occult Science,* written by Rudolf Steiner in 1909. In this chapter entitled, "The Present and Future of Cosmic and Human Evolution," Steiner writes:

> A knowledge thus arose among these new initiates that included everything that was the subject of ancient initiation. But in the center of this knowledge there radiated the higher wisdom of the Mysteries of the Christ Event . . . The hidden knowledge flows, although quite unnoticed at the beginning, into the mode of thinking of the men of this period. It is only self-evident that, up to the present, intellectual forces reject this knowledge. But what must happen will happen, in spite of all temporary rejection.
>
> The hidden knowledge, which takes hold of mankind now and will take hold of it more and more in the future, may be called symbolically "the Wisdom of the Grail." If this symbol, as it is given in legends and myths, is understood in its deeper meaning, we shall find that it is a significant image of the nature of a new initiation path which has the Christ Mystery at

its center. Modern initiates may, therefore, also be called the "Initiates of the Grail."

> A way into the supersensible worlds, the first stages of which have been described in this book, leads to the science of the Grail . . . What may be known through Imagination, Inspiration and Intuition about the higher worlds in connection with the Christ Mystery, will increasingly permeate the thought, feeling and will life of humanity. The concealed knowledge of the Grail will gradually be revealed; as an inner force, it will permeate more and more the manifestations of human life . . . We see that the highest imaginable ideal of human evolution results from the knowledge of the Grail: the spiritualization that man acquires through his own efforts.

The gradual revelation of this new path of initiation, based on the Grail knowledge, has come under the domain of the Archangel Michael whose regency began in 1879. Interestingly enough, 1879 also marks the year in which Wagner completed his *Parsifal* music drama, as was discussed in a previous chapter.

What is the significance of this new Age of Michael which began in 1879, and how can we characterize this guiding spirit? An age under the regency of one of the leading archangels lasts for about as many years as there are days in a year, that is about 365. The last Age of Michael was during the Golden Age of Greece. When considering both that age and our own, it is clear that the characteristics of a Michaelic Age may be described as cosmopolitan and international. Michael is not interested in nationality, race, creed, or in the hereditary background of an individual. As a Sun Being, he directs his gaze to what is essentially human and individual within every human being, whatever his/her background may be. His reign signifies a period of greater freedom, of greater independence. It is also a time when inspiration from the spiritual world decreases, and the human being is very much left to make choices in freedom. For Michael does not inspire. He waits for souls to turn to him, and only then (in as much as they do so) can he grant strength.

It is important to understand the role that the present Michaelic Age has in the development of the consciousness soul, a stage or epoch of human evolution which Steiner tells us began in the year 1413 AD and will take over 2,000 years to complete.

Rudolf Steiner never tired of characterizing the nature of the present epoch of human development as that of the consciousness soul. (When addressing English-speaking audiences, however, he recommended the term "spiritual soul," thinking that this was a more accurate translation.) What are the attributes of the consciousness soul? How is this stage of development different from the past? And how will these characteristics be reflected in the evolution of the individual and in the overall consciousness of humanity?

One of the most important contributions that Rudolf Steiner made to the study of history is to have pointed out that every age or epoch offers the possibility of acquiring new dimensions of consciousness. If we wish to understand the attributes of the age of the consciousness soul, it is helpful to contemplate the two previous ages as well—the age of the sentient soul and the age of the intellectual soul.

The age of the ancient civilizations of Egypt, Chaldea, Babylonia and the Holy Land began as the Great Pyramids of Egypt were being completed in 2907 BC. During this period of development, the sentient or feeling soul evolved. This state of consciousness allowed the men and women of that time to experience daily connection with the divine. Intellectualism as we know it today hardly existed. It was a period when the arts flourished in the service of religion. The people were guided by initiates who had acquired an insight into the spiritual world through a rigorous training in the Mysteries. Large populations who lived in the Middle East—the cradle of civilization—found their destinies in the ennoblement of their feeling life, especially in relation to other human beings and the surrounding world of nature.

A very different soul gesture was exhibited by the time Rome was founded in 747 BC and continued into the time of the Middle Ages as civilization moved west through the lands of the Mediterranean. This period encompassed not only the ancient Greek civilization and the rise of Arabism, but also the deed of Christ Jesus and the early centuries of Christendom. Steiner characterized this epoch as the development of the mind or intellectual soul. The

German term he used, *Verstandes- und Gemütsseele,* suggests that a particular relationship is established between the head and the heart as distinct from a dry intellectualism. This epoch, which lasted until 1413 AD, was a time when the intellect, the thinking power in man's soul, emerged with special strength. During this time, the Greek and Latin languages served as the principal instruments for the elaboration of philosophy and various forms of ritual. With the development of the intellectual or mind soul, the task of humanity became the overcoming of doubt, the establishment of faith, and the striving toward a golden mean.

The present age of the consciousness (or spiritual) soul dawned as the impulse of Joan of Arc was leading to the separation of England and France, as Jan Huss was questioning the authority of Rome and as the scientific age with its basis in exact perception began. It also was the time when Christopher Columbus and other navigators, through their daring deeds, established a global awareness that was to revolutionize man's relationship to himself, to others, to nature and to the heavens.

Increasingly mankind gained an ever-greater measure of freedom and independence in the earthly realm, as a living awareness of the spiritual realms faded into darkness. The right to question every aspect of life was born and, consequently, so was the anxiety associated with alienation. Since the Renaissance this separation from the knowledge of the spiritual world has continued to grow, and we increasingly rely on a technology devoid of spiritual and ethical values. This reliance has brought about a new temptation to value only the material, physical world, resulting in the exploitation of the resources of nature and the devaluation of the worth of the individual.

Since only 500 years of the consciousness soul epoch have elapsed, mankind will continue to struggle with these existential problems for another 1500 years. We are obviously struck by the painful, but necessary fact that the consciousness soul age, to begin with, appears to be a regression from the spiritual relationships that had been established in earlier times when the ideals of goodness, beauty and truth permeated mankind's striving both individually and in the body social. And yet, paradoxically, this age, out of its darkness and despair, will give rise to a new connection with the spirit based on individual experience achieved in full consciousness and freedom.

We stand at a dramatic threshold. The gods have taken a major risk and withdrawn. Will we as human beings awaken to our true task: to take responsibility for ourselves, for our relationships with one another, and for the survival of the earth? The future has been placed into our hands.

This then is the task of Michael: to help humanity develop the essential characteristics of the spiritual soul—a human consciousness that will bind the heavens and the earth in profound awareness and creative interplay. We can already see signs of this development as the loneliness, alienation, and separation from the spiritual world begin to cause souls to become weary and consciously to long for a spiritual reunion. Even the strong adherence to the material realm which humanity has had is beginning to lose its luster, encouraging many individuals to turn toward inner paths of development in search of spiritual awakening.

We are all men and women of the consciousness (spiritual) soul age, but the awakening—painful as it may be—can only occur individually. Though it has to be striven for, its achievement will yield a new sense of community both in the spiritual world and on Earth. The saga of Parzival with his many trials and tribulations is of such immediate value precisely because it prophetically foreshadows the gradual awakening through dullness and doubt to the newly-to-be-acquired spiritual soul.

What we read of the Quest for the Holy Grail in the sagas of the twelfth and thirteenth centuries prefigures symbolically what can only be fully realized now and in the future, namely, the fully-developed consciousness soul. The Grail stories have re-emerged as powerful symbols which are influencing the hearts and minds of thousands. They can now be translated into conscious, light-filled understanding that quickens the heart and leads the will to insight and action. Every modern soul, in as much as he/she becomes conscious of a supersensible dimension of existence, is bound to go through the Parzival stages of dullness and doubt, ultimately to arrive at *Saelde,* or blessedness, as illustrated in the previous chapter.

Let us return to some of the passages referring to

the Grail in the sixth chapter of *Occult Science,* so as to characterize still further the age in which we live.

> Then came the dawning of the present epoch known as the Fifth, which began in 1413, the character of which may be described as follows. In the first place the powers of man's intellect go on developing and will continue in doing so to an unprecedented extent both now and in the future.

This has become a common experience for every soul in the western world, and yet thinking, as we shall see, can also become the basis for supersensible experience.

> After the gradual preparation for this beginning slowly in the twelfth and thirteenth centuries AD, from the sixteenth century onward, the pace has been and is still rapidly accelerating. Thus the Fifth Epoch has become a period of human evolution ever more given up to the cultivation of intellectual powers, while the traditional knowledge of the past loses its hold upon the human soul.

This is an important point. Something new is emerging and we are losing the old. Steiner then speaks of the hidden esoteric knowledge which was gradually lost and which is now becoming available again for humanity.

> It is a characteristic of this new initiation knowledge that, while its facts can only be

investigated with higher faculties of cognition, once investigated and discovered they are well able to be comprehended precisely by the faculties of mind and soul which the Fifth Epoch, that is the consciousness soul, has developed. These faculties will more and more find satisfaction and fulfillment in the higher knowledge. We are now living at a time when the higher knowledge needs to be far more widely received into the general consciousness of mankind than hereto. It is with this in view that the present book has been written. And as the cultural evolution of mankind absorbs the knowledge of the Grail, in the same measure will the spiritual impulse of the Christ Event become effective.

This hidden knowledge of the Grail will become manifest and grow to be a power in man's life, entering ever more fully into all the ways and walks of man.

And so we find that we are confronted with something that has flowed underground and that now is reappearing. We have already seen that it is doing so in many poems, books and references that we find in contemporary life. Some, such as Solshenytsin, Steinbeck and T. S. Eliot, use the imagery of the Grail quite consciously. Yet, to appreciate this re-emergence rightly, we shall have to go back to the source and discover the origins of these powerful imaginations that are all rooted in actual events.

One such source is *The High History of the Holy Grail* (recently published under the title *Joseph of Arimathea: A Romance of the Grail*) by Robert de Boron, preserved in only one hand-written manuscript which can be seen in the Bibliothèque Nationale in Paris. The manuscript itself dates from the end of the thirteenth century, but Robert de Boron composed this prose work around the year 1200. This work throws light on the origin of the Grail as related to the Mystery of Golgotha and the various surrounding events.

After a brief introduction, Robert de Boron takes us back to Paradise and the Fall. The pain which Adam and Eve experienced at having to descend to earth, no longer to roam in the light-filled Garden of Eden, is described graphically. Quite simply, we are told that in order to redeem mankind a God had to take on human form and that, through the baptism of Jesus of Nazareth in the Jordan by John the Baptist, this God, the Christ, was able to walk the earth. Robert de Boron tells us the story succinctly:

> In the days when God walked on earth and preached His faith, the land of Judea was subject to Rome and under Roman control, not the whole land but the part of it where Pilate ruled.

We are now introduced to Joseph of Arimathea, who was a secret disciple of Christ. He was an older man, who had for many years been a merchant and had traveled widely. It is said that his travels had taken him as far west as Cornwall, where Tintagel, the seat of the Arthurian Round Table, would later be located. We are further told that on a number of occasions, Joseph had done small favors for Pilate, but repeatedly he refused to receive anything in return. The crucifixion is now described.

> When Joseph heard the news, his anger and grief were immense. He hurried to Pilate and said, "I have served you for a long time together with my five horsemen, but have never received any payment. But, I shall never accept any reward for it unless you will give me a gift as you have always promised me. Give it to me for it is within your power.

And so Joseph requested the body of Jesus, who was wrongfully hung on the cross. Pilate was amazed that he asked for so small a gift and said.

> I expected and secretly believed that you would want something of more value and certainly I would have granted it to you. Since you ask for His body, you shall have it as payment of your wages.

Hurrying back to the Hill of Golgotha, Joseph tells the Roman soldiers that Pilate had given him permission to take down the body. The soldiers, however, refused to accept his word, saying that they would release the body only if Joseph had the order in writing. Joseph returned to Pilate who gave him the written request as well as the chalice which had been taken from Christ upon His arrest. Fearing future recrimination for the Holy Man's death, Pilate wished to rid himself of anything which might later be used to incriminate him. Joseph readily accepted the vessel which had held the Sacrament during the celebration of the Last Supper.

Another legend, which is not part of Robert de Boron's story but was contemporary to it, tells us in an imaginative way of the cosmic origin of the Grail: During a great war in heaven, Michael and his angels fought against the hosts of Lucifer. As the battle raged, Michael struck the crown of Lucifer and from it a precious stone of great price fell to the earth. It was then fashioned into a vessel which eventually came into the possession of the Queen of Sheba.

The Queen carried the chalice to Jerusalem (around 1000 BC) and offered it as a gift to Solomon, thinking that they would be wed. The chalice was then handed down from generation to generation with great reverence, until it eventually appeared on the table of the Last Supper in the Upper Room, where Christ used it to celebrate the first communion saying, "This is my body; this is my blood." Then from the vessel He gave His disciples the bread and the wine.

After the celebration had been completed and Christ Jesus had been taken prisoner by Roman soldiers in the Garden of Gethsemane, the vessel fell into the hands of Pilate for a short time until it was given to Joseph of Arimathea.

In *The High History of the Holy Grail,* Robert de Boron tells us that upon receiving the cup and the official authorization to take Christ's body, Joseph immediately returned to Golgotha, where a portion of the blood that flowed from the wound in the right side of Christ Jesus was collected, thereby transforming the vessel into the Holy Grail. The rest of His blood, Robert de Boron tells us, flowed into the earth. After these events, which are described in the most moving way, we read of Christ's Entombment, Descent into Hell, and Resurrection.

Soon after the Resurrection, a large-scale persecution of Christ's followers begins. Some Christians were able to escape from Jerusalem, but Joseph of Arimathea was captured. He was placed, along with the Grail, into a high circular tower which was open to the sky. The soldiers then sealed him in and left him to die.

Robert de Boron's story continues forty years later in the city of Rome, where Titus, Emperor Vespasian's son, is dying of leprosy. After the last known remedy has failed to heal his son, Vespasian hears about an old woman named Veronica, who—so he is told—possesses a handkerchief with an engraved image of a countenance endowed with magical healing properties.

As mentioned in the previous chapter, when young, Veronica had witnessed Christ carrying His heavy cross along the Via Dolorosa in Jerusalem. In an effort to alleviate His pain, Veronica had placed her handkerchief softly on His face. As she removed it, she found to her amazement that the cloth was imprinted with His features. Later Veronica discovered that this cloth, which bore the most precious image of her Lord, now possessed astonishing powers of healing.

Our story continues as Veronica is summoned to bring her magical handkerchief to the palace. Upon her arrival she shows the cloth to the dying Titus whose face was in an advanced state of decay. To the wondrous amazement of Vespasian, his son was healed instantly. Filled with joy and awe, Vespasian and Titus implore Veronica to tell them about the man whose miraculous features were imprinted on the cloth. The old woman reveals to them that the image is that of Christ Jesus who had died on the cross in Jerusalem forty years ago.

Both the Caesar and his son departed immediately for Jerusalem, hoping to find others who had known the Christ. There they discovered the details of His fate at the hands of the Jews and the consequent persecution of His followers, most of whom were dead or had long fled the country. However, during their questioning, someone remembered the incarceration of Joseph of Arimathea in a tower near the place of Golgotha. Unsure of what they would find, Vespasian and Titus ordered ladders and ropes to be fetched with which the Roman soldiers managed to penetrate the top of the tower. There they found Joseph of Arimathea at the bottom of the tower, alive and well and holding the holy vessel. After his release, Joseph told his rescuers how he had been sustained these past forty years by the content of the holy vessel which magically replenished itself.

There is another wonderful legend, also contemporary to Robert de Boron's tale, which tells us that the wound in Christ Jesus' side, from which Joseph of Arimathea so reverently gathered his Lord's blood in the sacred chalice, was inflicted by Longinus, a Roman centurion. In order to make sure that the Crucified One had died, Longinus intended to thrust his spear into Christ Jesus' heart. However, due to an eye disease, he was unable to see clearly and pierced His right side instead. In doing so a few drops of Christ's blood fell on Longinus' eyes. He regained his sight and from that moment on he was able to see clearly with his heart as well as his eyes. As a result the centurion became a staunch disciple among a small band of early Christians. The image here is a poignant one which, when taken with Robert de Boron's tale of Joseph of Arimathea, adds another dimension to our understanding of the Holy Grail: not only does the Grail nourish each according to his needs, but the blood of Christ restores clarity of vision to both the eyes and the heart.

Continuing with Robert de Boron's story, we learn that Vespasian and Titus were overjoyed at having found the one surviving disciple of Christ Jesus and implored Joseph to tell them about Him. Thus they learned about many remarkable events in the life of our Lord. As their wonder and appreciation of Christ grew, so did their anger at the Jews for crucifying Him. In a moment of blind fury, Titus ordered the complete destruction of Jerusalem. A representation of the 70 AD annihilation of Jerusalem can still be seen today on the Titus Arch in Rome.

Robert de Boron now tells us that upon his release, Joseph had a profound spiritual experience.

In a dream, angels directed him to travel westward with the Grail until he found the place where his staff, when planted in the ground, would flower. It would be in this special place, he was told, where the Grail would find its home.

Joseph immediately departed from Palestine, accompanied by his sister, his brother-in-law, named Bron, and the three Marys: Mary Magdalene, Mary Cleophas, and Mary the Egyptian. This small band of early Christians, led by Joseph of Arimathea, sailed across the Mediterranean to France, where they landed near what is today Marseille.

(It is interesting to note that a small fishing village named Les-Saintes-Maries-de-la-Mer exists in that part of France. When Joseph of Arimathea left France for England, Mary the Egyptian returned to this area where she later died and was buried. It is here in this small village where a coffin, said to be that of Mary the Egyptian, can be seen suspended by ropes in the nave of the local church. Les-Saintes-Maries-de-la-Mer is well known today as a site of periodic gatherings of Gypsies, especially those from North Africa, who consider Mary the Egyptian as their patroness.)

After landing in France, Joseph's small party traveled further north along the Rhone valley, passing by Vezelay where, Robert de Boron tells us, Mary Magdalene would later be buried. Here in Vezelay, the Basilica of Mary Magdalene—still one of the finest Romanesque churches in western Europe—was built in her honor.

Joseph and his companions eventually arrived in

Chartres. The beauty of the site and the worship of the Black Madonna, a pre-Christian Celtic ritual by then already in decline, was so inspiring that Joseph sent a messenger to Ephesus to ask Mary the Mother for permission to dedicate the place to her. This is to be taken imaginatively, as Mary the Mother had actually died at an earlier date. It was with this dedication, as Christian tradition has it, that Chartres was first connected with Christianity. And thus, Chartres is also interwoven into the Grail Stream.

The story continues as Joseph, having left the three Marys in France and accompanied only by his sister and brother-in-law, crosses the Channel to England. As the staff still would not flower, they proceeded further west until they reached Glastonbury in Somerset, which at that time was an island within the island of Great Britain. There Joseph planted his staff and it flowered.

Today a rare thornbush, otherwise unknown in Europe, but common in the Middle East, can still be seen at Glastonbury, where it is said to have grown out of Joseph of Arimathea's staff. Many traditions surround the Chalice Well in Glastonbury in which the Grail Cup is said to have been hidden. Legend has it that, when humanity will have reached a measure of insight into the spiritual world, the Chalice will be found at the bottom of the well.

Robert de Boron now tells us that Joseph's sister and brother-in-law settled in the area and eventually had twelve sons, the youngest of which was called Alain or Alanus in Latin. Contrary to the custom of passing legacies onto the oldest son, it was Alain who became the first guardian of the original Grail community.

As with most legends, we are faced with the perplexing dilemma of determining how much of this story is based on historical events. We certainly find it rich in threads weaving into our present considerations. For instance, Robert de Boron was a contemporary of Alanus ab Insulis (1128-1203), the last of the great Chartres Masters. One wonders whether Alanus knew of the story of Joseph of Arimathea and the founding of the first Grail community. It has been established that Alanus ab Insulis was not the name with which this great master was born. Might he have named himself Alanus of the Island after Alain, the first guardian of the Grail community? Whether or not that be the case, we can imaginatively picture Joseph of Arimathea's journey, said to have occurred shortly after 70 AD, as weaving the Grail Stream from the east into the western Celtic Mysteries of the Black Madonna, in the process transforming and dedicating the place of Chartres to the Virgin Mary and finally arriving at Glastonbury.

We find that the Holy Grail was carried into the pre-Christian Celtic world, which includes Ireland, the west coast of Scotland, Wales and the western part of England. For thousands of years before the Mystery of Golgotha, Hibernian Celtic initiates had nurtured a cosmic mystery wisdom connected with the elements and forces of nature. They had foreseen, through their spiritual connection with the elemental forces of wind and weather, thunder and lightning, the roaring ocean, gazing in fire, in air and in water, that the cosmic Christ Being would incarnate in a body born of a virgin.

When Joseph of Arimathea brought the Holy Grail into the Hibernian Celtic Stream, thus Christianizing it, something quite remarkable took place. The Christian impulse came to flourish within this stream in such a way that the knowledge of the *cosmic* aspects of the Christ became its focus. The Christ was known to Celtic Christianity not only as a being of heavenly origin, as a Sun Being, but was also experienced as the living Spirit behind and within the cosmos, the earth and all nature. Because Celtic Christianity was able to retain its earlier pre-Christian connection to cosmic spirituality, even as it embraced the Christ, it became possible for a particular mystery wisdom, dedicated to Michael, to emerge from this stream and carry out a destiny of world significance.

Rudolf Steiner tells us that in ancient times all human intelligence was, in fact, Cosmic Intelligence and was under the rulership of the Archangel Michael. In ancient times, human beings experienced thought as divine inspiration, which came from outside themselves, and not as something personally created within the individual. The concept of Intelligence was understood, *a priori,* to mean a manifestation of the divine. Since the earth began, Michael had administered this Cosmic Intelligence. However, after the Mystery of Golgotha, this Intelligence began to fall away from Michael. As the Christ left the Sun sphere and descended to earth, Intelligence fell gradually from Michael's grasp, until by the ninth century AD it had come to rest entirely within the souls of human beings on earth.

The Celtic Stream, even as it embraced Christianity, had never forsaken the cosmos. Because of this, as the strength of the Grail impulse increased (about the fifth century AD), it became possible for a group of men to appear who represented the cosmic forces in such a way that they were able to fulfill a world destiny.

These men were King Arthur and his Knights of the Round Table. They stood, with King Arthur as the Sun at their center and with each Knight so embodying the impulse of one of the zodiacal constellations, that together they could act as a twelvefold whole. The Holy Grail was the ideal toward which their vision ever turned and which guided their deeds. As a Michael community they fought to ensure Michael's continued dominion over Cosmic Intelligence; they struggled against the severence of intelligence from Michael. They strove against the old demonic forces and on behalf of civilization. This community fought longer than any other that Michael should remain regent over Intelligence.

This was the mission of the Arthurian Round and can in many ways be seen as the fruit borne in the West by Joseph of Arimathea's staff.*

But the Holy Grail travelled first from the East, and there is another stream, the Grail Stream, whose mission, also guided by Michael, stands in sharp contrast to that of the Arthurian Round. Here it is fully recognized that Intelligence is no longer cosmic, that what now streams downward must appear as "foolish"—like Parzival—and that Intelligence must now be sought on the earth.

It was the mission of the Grail Stream to prepare the hearts and minds of men and women, so that Michael could enter into them and within the individual once again be regent over Intelligence.

Let us conclude with a quotation from one of Rudolf Steiner's last lectures, given in Torquay on August 21, 1924, which can be found in *Karmic Relationships* , Volume 8.

> There . . . stands King Arthur's castle, where men still turn to the cosmic intelligence and where they strive to instill the intelligence belonging to the universe into civilization on earth. And [there] stands that other castle, the Grail Castle, where the intelligence is no longer drawn from the heavens but where it is realized that what is wisdom before men is foolishness before God and what is wisdom before God is foolishness before men.
>
> The impulse proceeding from this other castle . . . strives to penetrate the intelligence that is now no longer the cosmic intelligence; and so in olden times lasting on into the age when the Mystery of Golgotha takes place over in Asia, we find in the Arthur Stream the intense striving to ensure Michael's dominion over the intelligence, and the Grail Stream going out from Spain the striving, in which account is taken of the fact that the intelligence must in future be found on earth, since it no longer flows down from the

> heavens. The import of what I have just described to you breathes through the whole Legend of the Grail.

This passage may help us to understand the contrast between these two streams. In the next chapter we shall look particularly at the contribution made by Wolfram von Eschenbach in his *Parzival* and how this work, above all others, gives us an insight into the quest that is so crucial for our time.

* In the summer of 1924, towards the end of his active life, Rudolf Steiner went to Tintagel, accompanied by a few friends. There at Tintagel Steiner was able to read in the spiritual surroundings something of the quality of what had lived in that Arthurian Round. He wrote down his impressions as follows:

> We come from old impressive ruined castles.
> Here sat of old the ancient demon conquerors,
> Strengthening their leader's power through
> the starry twelve.
> The castles are in ruins;
> The astral world is mute.
> Yet spirit power still thrives about the cliffs
> And powerful soul-pictures storm out
> from the sea . . .
> Magically interchanging is the interplay
> of light and air
> That presses forcefully upon the soul,
> Even today, after three thousand years,
> Anew and out of the memory pictures
> of the elements...
>
> (from a letter to Albert Steffen, 1924, by Rudolf Steiner, translated from the German by Arvia MacKaye-Ege)

It was also at this time that Steiner gave a series of lectures on education in Torquay, entitled *The Kingdom of Childhood,* and three lectures to the members of the Anthroposophical Society relating to the karmic threads that connect the Grail Stream and the Arthurian Stream. He also spoke of the significance of Chartres in a new way. The public series of lectures he gave are of particular interest and published under the title *True and False Paths of Spiritual Investigation.* Here, too, he refers in detail to the Chartres Masters.

In the summer of 1929, towards the end of his active life, [illegible]

[illegible]

IMAGES OF INITIATION
The Macrocosmic Symbolism of Wolfram von Eschenbach

In order to enter into the essence of our theme, we shall compare the openings of the Grail stories as related by Chrétien de Troyes and Wolfram von Eschenbach.

Chrétien composed his saga in poetic form in Old French around the year 1180 AD, but was unable to complete it. His poem, which bears the title *Perceval le Gallois or The Story of the Grail* opens as follows.

> He who sows little reaps little,
> and let him who wishes to reap
> scatter his seed on ground
> that will yield him a hundredfold,
> for on poor earth
> good seed dries up and dies.
> Chrétien sows the romance,
> which he is beginning,
> in so good a place
> that he cannot fail
> to gain great profit,
> for he does it for the worthiest man
> in the empire of Rome;
> that is the Count Philippe of Flandres,
> who is of greater worth than Alexander was.

> Though Alexander is said to be a model,
> I will prove that he did
> not equal the Count,
> for he gathered in himself
> all the sins and vices
> from which the Count is pure and free.

A little later we hear that the Count gave him the book on which the story of the Grail is based. And Chrétien continues,

> It was in the season when trees bloom,
> bushes put forth leaves,
> meadows turn green,
> birds sweetly sing in their language at dawn,
> and all things are aflame with joy.
> That the son of the widowlady
> of the lonely wild forest
> arose and easily saddled his hunter,
> took three javelins,
> and thus left his mother's manor,
> thinking that he would go
> to see his mother's harrowers,
> who were harrowing her oats
> with twelve oxen and six harrows.
> So he entered the forest
> and at once his heart rejoiced
> at the sweet season
> and at hearing the warbling of the birds.
> All these things pleased him
> and filled him with the sweetness
> of the calm weather.
> He took the bridle from his hunter
> and let him graze the fresh greening grass.

And a little later we find Perceval,

> the noble youth heard but did not see
> those who were approaching at a rapid pace.
> He wondered and said,
> "By my soul, the lady, my mother, told me
> the truth when she said
> that devils are the most terrible thing in the world
> and taught me that one ought
> to cross oneself against them.
> But, I scorn her teaching
> and will not cross my self,
> rather I will strike the strongest
> with one of the javelins I am carrying
> so that none of the others, I think,
> will dare to come near me.

Thus we meet the innocent, pure fool Perceval who believes he can fend off devils with javelins. Chrétien mentions that he received the story from Philippe, Count of Flandres, who was a much admired nobleman of the period. The Count promoted many of the troubadours and bards that travelled about the countryside singing and reciting romances, such as *Tristan and Isolde, Aucassin et Nicolette* and *Sir Gawain and the Green Knight.*

Similarly this story, as told by Chrétien de Troyes, became part of the illustrious repertoire of the *Minnesänger,* the great entertainers of the Middle Ages who delighted rich and poor, peasant and craftsmen alike. Their beautiful art of singing and recitation moved the hearts of countless audiences as they unfolded colorful adventures full of chivalry and virtue.

A generation later in 1213 AD, Wolfram von Eschenbach, who described himself as illiterate, finished dictating the sixteen books of his grand poem, *Parzival*, in Middle High German. The completed story contains an interweaving of philosophical and macrocosmic aspects involving over 200 characters. By contrast, in Chrétien's rendition we find relatively few characters, with hardly any mentioned by name, and an emphasis on detail underlining a microcosmic view.

Wolfram's opening is very different from Chrétien's. It has from the outset profound philosophical implications clothed in images and metaphors. As the drama begins, the contrast between black and white, heaven and hell becomes immediately apparent:

> If inconstancy is the heart's neighbor,
> the soul will not fail to find it bitter.
> Blame and praise alike befall,
> when a dauntless man's spirit is black and white
> mixed like the magpies' plumage.
> Yet, he may see blessedness after all,
> for both colors have a share in him,
> the color of heaven and the color of hell.
> Inconstancy's companion is all black
> and takes on the hew of darkness,
> while he of steadfast thoughts clings to white.
>
> This flying metaphor will be
> much too swift for dullards.
> They will not be able to think it through
> because it will run from them like a startled rabbit.
> Mirrors coated on the back with tin

and blind men's dreams,
these catch only the surface of the face
and that dim light cannot steadfastly endure,
even though it may make fleeting joy real.
Anyone who grabs the hair
in the palm of my hand where there isn't any,
has indeed learned how to grab close.
And if I cry Ouch! it will only show
what kind of a mind I have.
Shall I look for loyalty precisely
where it vanishes as fire,
in running water, dew in the sun?

A little later Parzival is introduced in an oblique way and not yet by name.

A brave man slowly wise—
thus I hail my hero—sweetness to women's eyes
and yet to women's hearts a sorrow,
from wrongdoing a man in flight!
The one whom I have thus chosen is,
storywise, as yet unborn.
He of whom this adventure tells
and to whom many marvels dare befall.

We thus hear of Parzival before his birth, as Wolfram describes the story of Gahmuret, Parzival's father, in the first book. Gahmuret first marries Belacane when he is in the East, serving the Baruch. This union results in a son by the name of Feirefiz who, we are told, is in fact half black and half white.

Gahmuret returns to the West where he meets and subsequently marries Herzeleide. Their union is, however, a brief one, as the restless nobleman, unable to live up to the steadiness symbolized by the anchor on his shield, decides once again to return to the East. Unaware that Herzeleide is pregnant with their son, the future Parzival, Gahmuret returns to the East and is slain there under dramatic circumstances.

The sweep of Wolfram's story from the outset links East and West. The Moorish woman, Belacane, her son, Feirefiz, and the Baruch represent the East, with Herzeleide and Parzival representing Western culture.

The heart of Wolfram's saga revolves around the fact that when Parzival finds himself in the Grail Castle, he completely misses the reason for his being there. Still very much the pure fool, Parzival remains a dullard, not knowing his true name, unaware that his mother has died, and ignorant that he has a father who is now in the spiritual world. He stands motionless in the Castle as he witnesses Amfortas, the ailing Grail King, who can neither stand, sit nor lie down due to a wound he received as a result of succumbing to sensual forces. At this point in his life, Parzival lacks the compassion, the fellow-feeling, the *Mitleid* (to use the German word which means *suffering-with*) to ask the healing question, "Uncle, what ails thee?"

Parzival's dullness causes anguish to all the noblemen and ladies in the Grail Castle who know that if only the pure fool would freely ask the question, their King would be healed of his terrible, festering wound. While present in the Grail Castle, Parzival witnesses the holiest of rituals enacted, the Grail ritual, where he sees the bleeding spear and the

Grail Vessel which was carried by Repanse de Schoye, the beautiful Grail Bearer. During the ritual, Parzival remains silent, dumb-founded, immobile. After the celebration has come to an end, he is given a room and passes the night tossing and turning, pursued by nightmares.

When Parzival wakes up in the morning, the castle is empty. He finds his horse below, saddled, and, after searching in vain for his host and the knights and ladies of the castle, Parzival jumps on his horse and rides out over the drawbridge. As he does so, it is lifted by some invisible hand, and his horse barely has time to jump over the moat. Once he has landed safely on the other side, Parzival hears a voice from the castle calling to him,

> Ride on and bear the hatred of the sun.
> You are a goose.
> If you had only moved your jaws
> and asked your host the question!
> But you weren't interested in winning great honor.

Let us pause here for a moment and consider the symbolic use of certain birds during the Middle Ages as denoting an esoteric ladder of development. The goose signifies the lowest rung. Here consciousness is earthbound. The silly goose, who is unaware of the realities of the supersensible world, is still fettered to only those aspects of life which are visible and audible to its senses. Thus we see that Parzival, despite his many adventures, is still at the very beginning of his path of inner development (the goose stage).

The next stage of esoteric development was represented by the peacock. A proud, haughty bird which only shows the fullness of its plumage, studded with hundreds of eyes, from time to time. The symbol of the peacock, therefore, corresponds to the acquisition of Imaginative Consciousness—a state of consciousness which allows one to see into the spiritual world in a new way. This stage, often referred to as clairvoyance, no longer requires the use of the physical eyes, but instead is able to use the spiritual organs of sight.

A further step is found in the swan. The signet who is grey and ugly grows into a stately, regal bird that glides upon the water with an unequalled white purity and grace. In fables, the swan provided its final symbolism shortly before death, when it sang out its once-in-a-lifetime "swan song." Symbolically, this is an image of the next level of spiritual awareness, Inspiration, or clairaudience.

The ultimate, highest level of spiritual awareness is known as Intuition. Not limited to seeing as in the case of Imagination, or to hearing as with Inspiration, Intuition is a condition of being totally at one with the reality of the spiritual manifestation, of being at one with its essence. This stage is represented symbolically by the pelican, which is the root of the name Belacane. It was believed that this remarkable bird, if unable to find food, would sustain the life of its young by piercing its breast with its beak and offering its own blood for their nourishment. In the Middle Ages the pelican, which symbolizes the ultimate sacrifice, was often used to represent the Christ.

Wolfram uses the two castles which are highlighted in the story as another element of symbolism. The first, the splendid Grail Castle, stands high atop a mountain in a thickly wooded area with a clear lake at its foot. It is a castle which is difficult to find but easy to leave.

In sharp contrast there is the Castel Merveil, the Castle of Wonders, the home of Klingsor the Black Magician. This castle, which is visible for miles around, is situated in southern Europe in the desert region of western Sicily. It is easily discovered, but once one has entered its inviting gate, all freedom to leave is lost. Here in this castle of black magic, Klingsor holds thousands of women prisoners. And it is here in the Castle of Wonders that another of the story's main characters, Gawan, confronts the forces of evil unleashed by Klingsor against the Grail Knights.

Now the events of the Grail story should not be seen merely as physical reality in the sense-perceptible world. We shall have to distinguish clearly between the different levels of consciousness.

We have already seen that initiation, sleep, and death are connected. The initiate is the one who, while still on earth, gradually awakens to the experiences of sleep. By crossing the threshold between the physical and the spiritual worlds while living, he experiences what happens after death. For him, the aphorism of Novalis, the German Romantic poet (1772-1801), has become a reality: *When a human being is born, he dies to the spirit, and when he dies, he is born into the spirit.*

It may be helpful to add that the Greeks spoke of sleep as the younger brother of death. When we are asleep, we unconsciously enter the same realm as those who have died. When we awaken the next morning, we may have intimations in dream pictures of having been united with those who have passed on before us, but as a rule we lack the clarity and the presence of mind to grasp fully the meaning of such spiritual encounters.

Initiation is a process of inner training which expands our consciousness to the extent that the knowledge and reality of the spiritual world can be integrated into every aspect of our conscious waking life. An initiate can enter the realm of sleep knowing and recognizing gradually that, at a different level, he has crossed the threshold into the world of those who have died.

Initiation, sleep (dream life), and death are intimately connected. The initiate has achieved a continuity of consciousness in sleep and has died before actually dying. Hence, the saying by Angelus Silesius, *If you do not die before you die, you perish when you die.*

In order to fulfill their destinies, both Parzival and Gawan are called upon to awaken from their sleep, their dream-like consciousness. To begin with, Parzival is unable to do this, as his inability to ask the question that would have healed Amfortas clearly reflects. Gawan, on the other hand, stands the test and is able to overcome Klingsor and liberate the prisoners in the Castle of Wonders.

Gawan's ordeals include having to maintain

himself on a rolling bed which is violently flung from one side of the room to the other; confronting a ferocious lion; and withstanding the onslaught of a multitude of arrows which are hurled at him. Gawan's experiences are dream-like in character. For example, the ordeal with the lion symbolically points to a trial of the heart which the lion represents.

Unlike Gawan who awakens early to his destiny, Parzival's failure to ask the question in the Grail Castle reflects a dullness and lack of presence of mind which could be likened to being asleep in consciousness even when awake in the world.

In fact, as the story unfolds, the three heroes of the Grail saga can be seen as representatives of three paths of cognition: Parzival, the Western man, needs to awaken through dullness and doubt to certainty of insight. Gawan is the man of the middle realm of the heart, the healer who is rich in feelings. Thus, in finding his balance, Gawan is able to deal with the forces of evil unleashed by Klingsor. And Feirefiz, Parzival's half-brother, represents the wealth of wisdom of the Orient that still lives with pristine power in the atavistic realm of the will. He represents the man of action who is as yet unable to see the Grail, but instead falls in love with the Grail Bearer, Repanse de Schoye. Symbolically, the three characters are one and represent the quest for the Grail in thinking, feeling and willing.

Rudolf Steiner speaks again and again of the fact that modern mankind is collectively beginning to cross the threshold. Will humanity awaken to the reality of the spiritual world—a world that is as active and as manifold as the physical reality that surrounds us? The individual, too, is facing this threshold, often unprepared and in confusion of soul.

Sooner or later, every modern human being is called to face the abyss; and it appears as if his soul forces of thinking, feeling and willing are torn in three different directions. What he thinks is not in tune with his feelings; and he is unable to carry into action (deed) what he feels or thinks; or he does something that is estranged from both his conscious understanding and his feeling life. This condition where the head and the heart are at odds, can be seen as a form of schizophrenia which, as Steiner tells us, will become more prevalent as we approach the new millennium.

In the Grail story this struggle is expressed pictorially when Parzival (the man of the head) meets Gawan (the man of the heart) and a struggle ensues. However, Gawan, the feeling man, knows how to deal with the situation and their quarrel is resolved. It is at this point that Gawan takes over the story's major focus as he finds his way to Klingsor and the Castle of Wonders.

Later in the story after many experiences of pain and doubt, Parzival gradually begins to awaken. Finally, he finds himself riding through the countryside in full armor on Good Friday. While riding, he experiences extreme cold and then intense heat. Although he is unaware of the holiness of this day, these experiences kindle a poignant personal realization in his soul, and the suffering of Christ Jesus on the cross becomes Parzival's own suffering.

This dramatic turning point leads him by a gift of destiny to meet Treverizent, the Grail teacher, with whom he remains for two weeks in a secluded hermitage. There Parzival receives the deepest insight into the Mysteries of the Holy Grail.

Though the characters are still separated physically, Parzival and Gawan have become united, as are the head and the heart. It is at this point that Parzival has a terrible confrontation with his half-brother Feirefiz. At first they do not recognize one another and engage in a struggle to the death. Fortunately, before the fatal moment, each awakens in recognition, and it is as if Parzival is now for the first time united with his own will.

When finally Parzival has grown sufficiently to be worthy to become the Grail King, he is told that one cannot go to that holy place alone. When he choses his half-brother Feirefiz, the great drama finds its resolution: The path from the individual to the community, from separateness and alienation to union and togetherness, is accomplished. The powers of insight, the warmth of the heart, and the determination of the will are brought together in the service of the highest ideal.

THE ETERNAL FEMININE
From Kundry to Sigune

As we have seen, the Grail stories can be considered from a number of different aspects. Upon reflection we find that the theme of love in its manifold levels and stages weaves a golden thread throughout all the adventures. In fact, the Quest for the Holy Grail is a pilgrimage on the path of love that leads ultimately to the realization of the highest ideal.

Of the many characters portrayed in the romance, seven women play archetypal roles in the quest. Each one is connected more or less intimately with one or more of the three heroes of the story: Parzival, Gawan and Feirefiz. Though each man has his own individual destiny, they nevertheless form a unity.

Parzival is on a quest of cognition at both an individual and a universal level. Gawan is the feeling man who develops wondrous powers of healing. Feirefiz, who is half black and half white, is the man of action. The threefoldness in their characteristics reminds us of the three kings who come to the newborn Jesus Child in the Gospel of St. Matthew. In the Grail sagas, it is the resurrected Christ around whom they gather.

Within Wolfram's story, it is not until Parzival, Gawan and Feirefiz have undergone mutual struggle, acknowledged each other, and then formed a union with one another that a miracle occurs and Parzival becomes a whole human being—balanced and united in thinking, feeling and willing—able to fulfill his mission and become the new Grail King. Together these three characters thus form the archetype of the mystery of the new communion: *For where two or three are gathered in my name, there am I in the midst of them.*

But this mystery could never be accomplished without the seven women who could be said to represent the seven colors of the rainbow. Through the pain they suffer and the ideals they represent, they help to build a bridge from the sensible to the supersensible world.

Let us consider in turn Sigune, Herzeloyde, Belacane, Condwiramurs, Orgeluse, Repanse de Schoye, and Kundry, by characterizing each one briefly.

* * *

As we saw in Chapter One, Sigune is the woman whose special gifts allow her to read the cosmic script. This script was inscribed in precious stones on the leash of a dog given to her by her beloved, Schianatulander. We recall that Schionatulander's name implies that he was the messenger of Isis, the goddess who sits at the source of the Egyptian Cosmic Mystery Wisdom. It was his task to bring this knowledge down to earth for Sigune to interpret. In this saga Sigune represents the human soul who is striving to learn the cosmic wisdom of the stars.

Unfortunately, the escape of the dog with his leash and the slaying of Schionatulander by Orilus prevent Sigune from completing her task. "Carrying all these things in her heart," Sigune appears in the story, with her dead lover in her arms. We are here reminded of the *Pieta*,the sensitive sculpture executed by the young Michelangelo which depicts the Mother of Jesus holding her dead son in her lap.

Sigune plays a profound role in the unfolding of the saga. For it is her task to help Parzival awaken to his true destiny. As was mentioned in our considerations of Joseph of Arimathea and King Arthur, by the ninth century when the events of this saga took place, the ancient mystery wisdom represented by Sigune and Schionatulander had ebbed away, no longer able to come to the earth. Thus we see the significance of Sigune's and Schionatulander's premature deaths, for she also dies at a young age.

Sigune's role in Parzival's destiny can be seen as a poignant gesture of the old mysteries giving birth to the new. Before she dies she stirs in Parzival the beginnings of the new mystery wisdom—that wisdom of *Saelde* or *blessedness* which is found at the core of the new Christ Mysteries. The first thing Sigune does to awaken Parzival is to tell him his true name which has in its very essence the nature of his personal struggle. She also tells him that he is a king and will someday wear a crown on his head and that Schionatulander died defending the kingdom which belonged to Parzival but of which Parzival was unaware. Finally, she confronts him with the fact that, while in the Grail Castle, his continued dullness and insensitivity prevented him from asking the question which could have healed the ailing Anfortas.

* * *

Herzeloyde, Queen of Waleis and Nogals, the second wife of Gahmuret and mother of Parzival, shares a common destiny with Sigune, for both of them lose their true loves. Not only do they share this common sorrow, but we find that they are, as indeed are most of the characters in the Grail story, also related by blood: Herzeloyde is Sigune's aunt.

We recall that Gahmuret loved Herzeloyde deeply but was too restless to stay with her long. Soon after their marriage, unaware that she was pregnant with his son, Gahmuret leaves on a journey to the East where he is brutally slain. The tragic news of his death is imparted to Herzeloyde by Schionatulander who was then a young page in Gahmuret's service. Henceforth, the path of Herzeloyde is one of sorrow.

During her pregnancy, Herzeloyde has many a troublesome dream about the child she is to bear, and therefore awaits the moment of birth with great trepidation. From the moment of his birth, Parzival's mother does everything she can to hide from him his true origin. She only calls him by endearments such as "Beau Fils, Cher Fils, Bon Fils," never by name.

Overly possessive and overprotective, Herzeloyde wishes to spare Parzival the fate of her late husband, who was tragically killed in the service of knighthood. However, all of her efforts are in vain, for the day comes when she has to watch her young son ride off in pursuit of the very profession that killed her beloved. As we know, the loss of her only child along with the earlier death of her husband cause Herzeloyde more "heart's sorrow" than she can bear, she swoons and dies just as Parzival is disappearing from sight.

Herzeloyde, whose very name signifies "heart's sorrow," portrays in a most moving way the suffering of a wife who has lost her husband and of a mother deprived of her son. Later, through an awareness of her death and the role he played in bringing it about, Parzival reaches a new level of consciousness and experiences remorse.

* * *

We now turn to Belacane, the Queen of Zasamanc. We find that the destiny of Gahmuret's first wife and mother of Feirefiz is one of fortitude and sacrifice. This black woman of the East represents the intuitive wisdom of the Orient. Though not yet Christianized, Belacane, whose name is derived from Pelican or "Pelicane" possesses the virtues of the faithful, sacrificing heart.

We see from the beginning of the story that it is Belacane's misfortune to fall in love with Gahmuret. Though he marries and begets her with child, Belacane fears that Gahmuret will not stay with her. During her pregnancy, Gahmuret leaves her and returns to his home in the West. Before he departs, he vaguely promises Belacane that, if she should become a Christian, they would remain united—a condition he never gives her the opportunity to fulfill.

Abandoned by her husband, Belacane devotes her life to the care of her young child Feirefiz who, she senses, has a great destiny waiting for him in the West. This destiny is realized when Feirefiz, who is part black and part white, is selected by his half-brother Parzival to accompany him to the Grail. As the representative of the wisdom of the Orient, Belacane can be seen as key to Parzival's relationship to the East. As mother of Feirefiz, it is she who leads the splendor of the intuitive wisdom of the East to meet the conscious path of the West.

* * *

Now let us briefly consider the three women who become the wives of the three principal heroes of our tale: Condwiramurs, Duchess Orgeluse de la Lande and Repanse de Schoye.

Condwiramurs, Parzival's wife whom he marries early in the story, lives up to the meaning of her name which is derived from the French *conduire à l'amour*—the one who leads to love. And indeed we find that their union is a perfect one, in spite of the fact that Parzival's adventures take him away for long periods of time. Parzival comes to an inner experience of love through the love of Condwiramurs.

From the very outset they seem destined for one another and their relationship has a well nigh idyllic character. Together they have two sons: Loherangrin, the Swan Knight, and Kardeiz. Loherangrin in particular carries his father's ideals farther West. In fact there are a number of legends in the Netherlands and the eastern part of England that tell of his healing intervention, especially in social affairs. Loherangrin is credited with having founded free towns independent from serfdom and feudalism.

* * *

Gawan's wife, the Duchess Orgeluse de la Lande, embodied fully the meaning of her name which was derived from the French *orgueilleuse de la lande*—the proud one on the heath. She was indeed a shrew who made life unbearable for Gawan. However, the key to her role is finally revealed towards the end of the story when Orgeluse tells Gawan that she was sent to him by destiny in order to make his life difficult. By working to tame Orgeluse through compassion, tolerance and love, Gawan was able to develop the strength of character needed to fulfill his true task: that of confronting Klingsor, the Magician, in the Castel Merveil.

* * *

Répanse de Schoye, the wife of Fierefiz, is a young woman of great beauty and nobility in the service of the Grail. It is her role to carry the precious Grail vessel during high celebrations so that it may shine and bring joy to all who partake of its nourishment. Thus we can see that her destiny in life reflects the meaning of her name which is derived from the French *celle qui répand la joie*—the one who spreads joy.

We have already discovered that many of the characters of the Grail saga are related by birth or marriage. Therefore, it is not surprising to find that Répanse de Schoye's lineage involves many of the Grail's major personalities including her father, Frimutel, who is also the father of Anfortas, Treverizent, and Herzeloyde, as well as the grandfather of Sigune and Parzival.

Répanse does not meet her future husband until the saga is approaching its climax. At this time, the stranger from the East enters into the Grail Castle. Though he is yet unable to see the Grail, Feirefiz is not blind to the beauty of Répanse de Schoye and immediately falls in love with the Grail Bearer. As a result of his union with Répanse and his having been chosen to accompany Parzival to the Grail, Feirefiz ultimately finds a deep connection to the living Christ.

The unification of Feirefiz, the one who represents the wisdom of the Orient, and Répanse de Schoye, the Bearer of the Grail, epitomizes the gradual influence of the Christ Mysteries throughout the world. The knowledge of the Christ deed, which is meant for all mankind, began to spread throughout the Orient with the journeys of St. Thomas, the disciple of Christ who is said to have travelled widely throughout China and India.

In the ninth century the Christ influence in the East was strengthened by the travels of Prester John or "Priest John," the son of Feirefiz and Répanse. It is Prester John who is said to have carried the Grail Mysteries to the Orient. It is significant to note that in the latter part of the fifteenth century many of the great Portuguese navigators sought to round the Cape of South Africa in order to discover the realms of Prester John, which were said to lie in the Far East.

The Grail Mysteries are to this day not yet recognized in the East. But the attempts emanating from St. Thomas and Prester John should be seen as powerful seeds for the future. For it is the promise of the Grail to feed all those who seek its nourishment, regardless of their race or creed.

* * *

In considering the seventh woman, Kundry, we meet one who is poignantly torn between the extremes of her sensual and spiritual nature. Wolfram describes Kundry as the sister of Malcreatiure, the evil creature, and as the messenger of the Grail.

It is Kundry who, in the service of Klingsor the Black Magician, seduces Anfortas thereby bringing about his ruin. And yet, even though she is enslaved by the dark forces of Klingsor, Kundry longs to serve the highest. She symbolizes the battle of the torn, restless and capricious soul who struggles to find health and harmony.

Much light is thrown on the riddle of Kundry's being when we take into account her previous incarnation as Herodias, the mother of Salome. Perhaps we can imagine that in her life between death and rebirth, Kundry remembered having seen the Christ and that, although she acted so despicably toward Him, spitting upon His countenance, the infinite goodness of his gaze nevertheless kindled a resolve in her being to seek to serve the highest in her next incarnation. Her role in the destiny of the Grail Knights is a profoundly difficult and essential one. It is she, as temptress, who gives the Knights of the Grail the opportunity to confront and overcome evil.

* * *

Thus, we see in the seven central female characters the fullness of womanhood. These abilities to bring beauty to life, to struggle to overcome evil, to love unconditionally, to suffer, to encourage and inspire, to give birth, to nourish and protect, to lead, to sacrifice are all expressions of the eternal feminine.

The significance of the Eternal Feminine cannot be understood in its essence without a reconsideration of the mystery of the Trinity. Tradition still speaks of the Father, Son and Holy Spirit without sufficient understanding of the spiritual gender involved. The world of the Father above, as the creative principle, is complimented by the Mother Spirit that comes from below and nurtures that which is created. The Mother is fundamentally connected with the earth; in fact, the word *matter* comes from *mater—mother*—the *matrix*. We might therefore re-envision the first person of the Trinity as the Father *and* Mother principle working jointly.

Seven Aspects of the Eternal Feminine

Sigune
Woman as reader
of the cosmic script

Condwiramurs
Woman as ideal
wife

Répans de Schoye
Woman as priestess

Herzeleide
Woman as sorrowful
widow

Balacane
Woman as noble
sacrifice

Orgeluse
Woman as shrew

Kundry
Woman as temptress
striving for redemption

R. M. Querido

The Son, the Christ, is masculine in nature, but the Holy Spirit, the Sophia, was experienced in earlier times as feminine. A pre-Christian foreshadowing of this being is found in Greek mythology as Pallas Athena. In esoteric Christian tradition we find that the Whitsun experience (Acts 2), where the Spirit descended upon the disciples and the first Christ-centered community was formed, could not have occurred without the presence of Mary the Mother. She is the Sophia, the mother of John/Lazarus, who embodies the archetype of the transformed Eve forces that leads mankind onward to the highest.

This imagination will continue to take on ever deeper meaning in the Age of Light. It offers a key to understanding why issues surrounding women and society have gained so much attention in our time. A more spiritual understanding will also guard against an all too materialistic interpretation of a delicate soul realm that is now seeking to be explored.

The Eternal Feminine is a concept that has many meanings. One of the most easily accessible is found in the fact that the human soul, whether living in a man or a woman, is feminine in nature. It is receptive, imaginative and nurturing. In the French, *l'âme* is feminine; equally in German, *die Seele* is also feminine.

Rudolf Steiner emphasized that the further development of the human being will not take place in or by the body, neither is it a question of developing the spirit, but further stages of consciousness will arise through the transformation of the soul forces. We are endowed with three such soul elements known as the sentient soul, that is the feeling soul; the mind soul, the seat of reasoning power; and the consciousness soul, the heart of our will nature.

In Christian tradition they were represented as the Three Marys and they can be seen in many a Russian Icon. It is particularly in that culture that an age-old tradition of the Holy Sophia in its threefold form was still kept, long after the Western concepts of the spiritual world lost their fullness.

In the words of Goethe,

Woman Eternal draws us on high.

The eternal feminine draws us upward from Kundry who struggles to free herself from the forces of darkness through sorrow, sacrifice and love, to Sigune who is able to read the cosmic script so that it may again become meaningful to everyday life on the earth.

* * *

Of the four gospels, John comes closest to mentioning the Grail Mystery, though he does not speak of the chalice as such. In John 19:32-40, we find the following:

> So the soldiers came
> And broke the first one's legs
> Then those of the other one
> Who was crucified with him

When they came to Jesus
And saw that he had already died
They did not break his legs
But one of the soldiers
Pierced his side with a lance
And blood and water
Came out immediately

He has borne witness
Who saw this
And his witness is true
And he knows
That he speaks the truth
So that you also may believe

For all this took place
In order that the Scripture
Might be fulfilled
No bone of him
Shall be broken

And again
Another Scripture says
They shall look on him
Whom they pierced
Now after all this
Joseph of Arimathea
Who was a disciple of Jesus
But had kept it secret
For fear of the Jews
Asked Pilate
If he might take the body of Jesus
And Pilate gave him leave

Nicodemus
Who had first come to Jesus at night
Came with him
And he brought a mixture of myrrh and aloes
Weighing about a hundred pounds

So they took Jesus' body
And bound it in linen sheets
With the spices
According to the burial custom of the Jews*

Shortly before this passage we find in John 19:26-27 how through one of the last words from the cross John becomes deeply connected with Mary the Mother, the Sophia, the eternal feminine.

When Jesus saw his mother
And the disciple whom he loved
Standing there
    He said to his mother
        Here is your son
    Then he said to the disciple
        Here is your mother

And from that hour
The disciple
Took her into his home*

Through the word of Christ, John and Mary were united as mother and son—a relationship which previously could have taken place only through a blood connection. This points to a possibility that will increasingly occur in the future: A new family, a new community will arise through the Christ. But this in itself implies that ever increasing numbers of human beings will give birth to the higher self within them. This birth of the higher self, out of the transformed forces of the astral body, can be expressed as arising out of the eternal feminine. This transformation is depicted in the sublime cosmic imagination of John the Evangelist in the twelfth chapter of *The Apocalypse of St. John*:

> Then a great portant became visible in the heavenly spheres: a woman clothed with the sun, with the moon under her feet, and a crown of twelve stars upon her head. Being pregnant, she cried out in her labour and in the pains of giving birth to her child.
>
> . . . And she gave birth to the son who is to shepherd all nations with a crook of iron.
>
> And her child was snatched away by God to his throne.**

Here we have a sublime picture of the eternal feminine giving birth to the new human being who will be able to fulfill the quest for the Holy Grail and enter the service of the highest on behalf of all the world.

* *The Gospel of John* as rendered in English by Kalmia Bittleston, Floris Books, 1984.

** From a translation by Alfred Heidenreich as found in *The Book of Revelation*, Alfred Heidenreich, Floris Books, 1977.

THE MYSTERY OF THE HOLY GRAIL
The Earth as a Living Organism

Man's survival on the Earth is threatened in a variety of ways. There are natural catastrophies such as hurricanes, earthquakes, and extended droughts which cause the suffering and deaths of hundreds of thousands of men, women and children. Such sudden, apocalyptic events can result in a transformation of consciousness in those who survive—a change born out of untold suffering. This new consciousness is often reflected in a more reverential attitude toward one's relationship with the Earth, one's fellow human beings, and life itself.

There are also slower, less spectacular threats to man's survival, and it is mainly with these that this chapter will attempt to deal. World population is increasing at an alarming rate as natural resources are becoming scarce and a variety of environments and species are seriously threatened. The question of whether the Earth is able to provide enough food, water and clean air to nourish additional millions every year is an immediate one.

Concern for the well-being of our planet, for the kingdoms of nature and their balanced interplay has been on the increase since the mid-fifties. In the thirties, forties and fifties warning signs were expressed by forerunners of the environmental movement, such as Rachel Carson and Fairfield Osborn. These two protectors of the Earth, along with a few others, pointed out man's appalling misuse of the Earth's resources. Unfortunately, their messages were not taken seriously.

Fairfield Osborn wrote two books, *Our Plundered Planet* and *Limits of the Earth,* in which he examined in a challenging way the problem of natural resources in relation to increased population. Though these books roused some interest at the time, their main message seems to have gone unheeded. By carefully reviewing the actual and potential resources of the world's principal food-producing countries, Osborn showed that mankind must bear the blame for the critical situation in which we find ourselves. Statistics from 1950 showed that there were 2,500 million people living on the Earth, and it was estimated that two-thirds to three-fourths were malnourished. Osborn was of the opinion that without a fundamental "change of heart" it would be impossible to stem the spread of famine over the face of the Earth. In what sphere must this "change of heart" take place? It lies in the sphere of mankind's relation to the Earth; mankind must recognize the necessity of co-operating with nature. Today the Earth has a population of five billion, and it is estimated that half to two-thirds are underfed—a clear indication that this problem is far from being solved.

One of the factors which has contributed to the alarming present-day situation is the world-wide spread of soil erosion. One can argue that it has always existed and that the ancients knew of it, yet the appalling level of recent devastation it has caused is a new factor since the beginning of this century. In fact, May 12, 1934 has become a historic date in this respect. On that day black clouds darkened the bright midday sun over Washington, DC. People asked what this meant. As the truth became known, the enormity of it seemed beyond grasp: throughout the Midwest, thousands of acres of top soil were being blown off the face of the Earth. In a matter of hours this once fertile land was reduced to vast barren stretches; hundreds of thousands of acres had become useless. The Dust Bowl was born and had come to stay. Upon investigation it was found that half a million acres should never have been plowed at all, but the damage was done and only humanity was to blame.

Although the Dust Bowl is perhaps the most spectacular example of soil erosion, the trouble is by no means confined to the United States. In fact, it would be true to say that no continent is free from it; not even Europe, where farming still tends to follow a more or less traditional pattern adapted to local conditions. Even here the lack of insight concerning proper treatment of the Earth is beginning to show its effects.

In the U.S. soil erosion on a large scale is primarily due to human greed. Where land was cheap the early settler made little effort to keep the soil in good condition through manuring, proper plowing and an adequate rotation of crops. He simply moved on as soon as he found that the yield of his crops was declining. Thus, waste land was created at an alarming rate; what was ruined by the recklessness of one person would take many generations to heal. Strip mining of cropland on a large scale for quick financial return is also responsible for a dramatic decrease in the amount of arable land.

Other threats to our soil include overgrazing by cattle, which hardens the ground and breaks the binding element in the soil, thus exposing it to the risks of wind erosion. The thoughtless cutting down of the rain forests of Costa Rica or the forests of the northwestern states reduces the water table, alters the local climate, adversely affects precipitation, and leaves the land unprotected from the raging elements; drought and barrenness are the unavoidable results. It is apparent that without large-scale recycling efforts and a more conscientious use of timber-based products, our gargantuan demands for paper will continue to deplete our forests at a devastating rate: a single edition of the New York Sunday Times swallows 60-80 acres of soft wood!

One further instance to characterize the situation: As a result of the erosion disaster in 1935, when the world at large became aware that the Earth's resources were being depleted, the Tennessee Valley Authority was established to preserve the Tennessee Valley, a threatened area of the U.S. Briefly, it was found that unless all industries in the Valley were prepared to work together, whether farmers or timber firms, little could be done to prevent a critical situation from taking its natural course to disaster. The farmers along the lower reaches of the river agreed to adopt identical methods of agriculture; however, the timber-people defended their own limited interests and refused to co-operate: as a result the total plan was seriously undermined.

It is obvious that practical fraternity must penetrate into all realms of economic life if we are to survive. This is well within our capacities, for as Osborn said, "The new geologic force is man." Mankind can choose to continue to be the plunderer, or he can choose to become the healer of the Earth. The problem of soil fertility and the need for increased food production to sustain an ever-growing population is not only one of science, agriculture and distribution; it becomes a question of ethics.

But if there is to be this radical "change of heart," much will depend on how mankind views the Earth. If he persists in merely regarding it as a conglomeration of dead matter whirling in space, without why or wherefore, nothing will be achieved.

Concerns about ecology, erosion, endangered species, polluted air and water grew into powerful movements after the mid-fifties. A younger generation—born largely after the Second World War—expressed in no uncertain terms that we, all of us, as world citizens bear a profound responsibility for the future of our planet. They cried out that Mother Nature, ignored for so long, was dying and that we were committing her murder.

As a result of this new consciousness, the ideals of holistic food, holistic medicine, and a holistic way of life in harmony with the rhythms of nature began to spread rapidly. During the sixties and the seventies these were implemented enthusiastically by the young in cheerful, determined crusades. The emphasis was placed on community effort, on cooperatives, on working and striving together, rather than on pursuing one's own individual ambitions. For the most part a selfless attitude prevailed in their attempts to save the earth.

Though their banner cries might appear more subdued in the 1990's, there still exists a determined desire to protect the Earth. For example, we have seen many cities and towns initiate curbside recycling services and many environmental groups still struggle to preserve wilderness areas. However, in order to be truly effective, these movements will require the support of ever- increasing numbers of people who are willing to value the well-being of the Earth more than financial gain.

Let us now consider how mankind's picture of the Earth has changed through the ages. The history of cartography, the science of map-making, affords an excellent means of study in this respect. It shows how the early representations of the Earth as divinely ensouled have given way to the modern, purely utilitarian world-projections of our age. One can do little more in the limited space of this chapter than deal with a few examples. Therefore, I have chosen to contrast and compare two world maps produced during the Middle Ages: one by a Moslem, the other by a Christian.

It is well known that during the Middle Ages, the Moslem world carried a transformed variation of the Greek impulse into a many of fields of knowledge.

This was reflected in the science of cartography where Arab mapmakers used projections showing latitudes and longitudes which had been established with a fair amount of accuracy.

Al-Idrisi, born in 1099, was doubtless the most remarkable cartographer of his time; a genius, greatly helped by circumstance, he travelled widely in Europe, Africa and Asia Minor, finally settling in Palermo at the court of Roger II, the Norman King of Sicily. This environment afforded him the opportunity he needed to write his geographical treatise, *For the Amusement of Him Who Desires to Travel Round the World*. He did not have to rely only on his own observations, for Roger II engaged navigators, merchants and others to supply a wealth of geographical material. Thus, shortly after Al-Idrisi completed his Celestial Sphere in 1154, the first "traveller's guide-book" was produced.

Although the plan of the maps was simple, the strongly analytical spirit of Al-Idrisi was clearly revealed. Each region was illustrated by a separate map showing latitudes and longitudes, and giving descriptions of climate, land formation, etc. These regional maps, when assembled, formed a rectangular map, with the Mediterranean area as its center, oriented toward the South. In other words, the Al-Idrisi map appears inverted; for the modern custom orients maps to the North, upwards.

The other map, called the Ebstorfer World Map, reveals a very different picture of the Earth. In 1830 this map, which was created as a fresco painted on the wall of the Michael Chapel in a monastery near

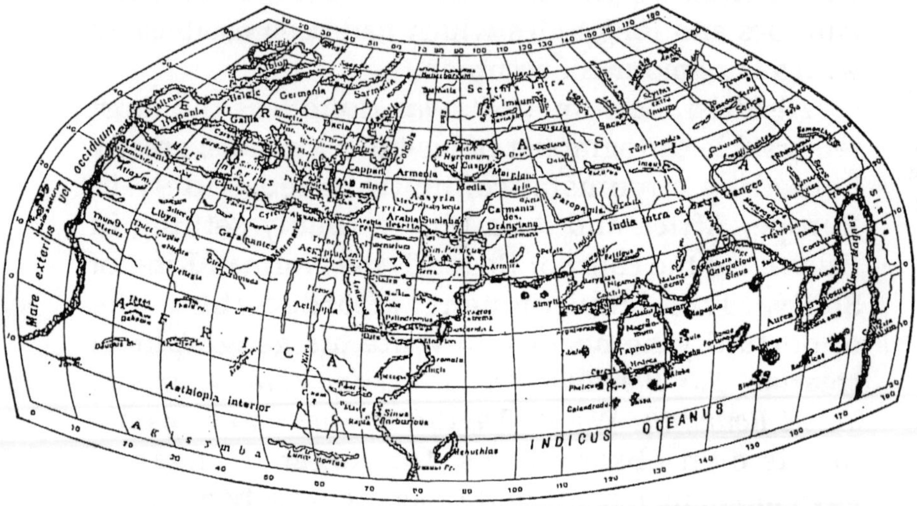
EUROPA
Germania
Sarmatia
Scythia intra Imaum
Hispania
Gallia
Dacia
Mare Internum
Mare occidentum vel Mare exterius
Armenia
Hyrcanum vel Caspium
Media
Assyria
Arabia Deserta
Arabia Felix
Carmania
Libya
Garamantes
Aegyptus
Aethiopia
AFRICA
Aethiopia interior
Agisymba
Sinus Barbaricus
Menuthias
INDICUS OCEANUS
India intra et extra Gangem
Gangeticus Sinus
Taprobana
Sinus Magnus
ASIA
Serica
Sacae

S

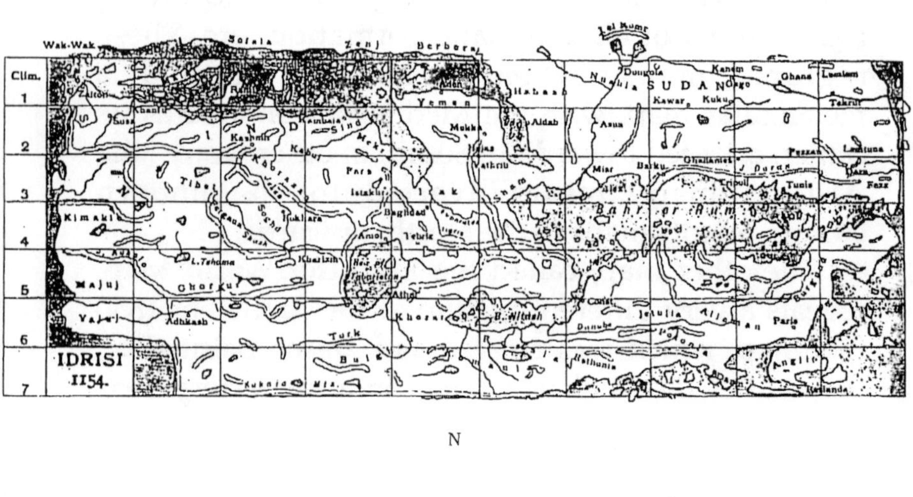
Wak-Wak
Sofala
Zenj
Berbera
Clim.
1
2
3
4
5
6
7
IDRISI
1154.
Aden
Yemen
Habash
Nubia
SUDAN
Dongola
Kanem
Ghana
Kawar
Kuku
Mukka
Aidab
Asua
Sind
Kashmir
Kabul
Fars
Tibet
Misr
Tunis
Fezzan
Lamtuna
Fazz
Tripoli
Bahr er Rum
Kimaki
Baghdad
Tebriz
Sham
Bukhara
Majuj
Yajuj
Khazizin
Adhkash
Turk
Khozar
Const.
Paris
Anglia
Irlanda
Danube

N

Hannover, Germany, by Gervasius of Tilbury, England (1160-1235), was rediscovered. It was richer and more important than any of the other *T in O* maps of the Middle Ages. Unfortunately, it was destroyed in a bombing raid during the Second World War, but reproductions reveal that it was about 13 feet in diameter, as opposed to the better known Hereford map which only measured 5 feet in diameter. It was also beautifully painted in 16 different colors forming an artistic whole which embodies a wealth of geographical, historical, and mythological detail.

The uniqueness of the Ebstorfer World Map lies in the fact that it represents the Earth as the Body of Christ. The map is oriented toward the East, showing the head of Christ and the four rivers of Paradise as lying within the Asian continent. His outstretched hands are depicted at either end of the horizontal beam, representing the Black Sea on the northern side, and the Nile on the southern side, with Jerusalem forming the center of the map. The foot region is shown at the bottom of the vertical beam represented by the Mediterranean Sea and to the far west are found the Pillars of Hercules.

To understand something of the significance of this map, we shall have to consider briefly the biography of Gervasius of Tilbury. He was related to the Plantagenets. In his youth he was friendly with Henry, son of King Henry II who shared with him a great love for the troubadours.

Gervasius showed remarkable ability as a young man and was allowed to be present at the Venice

Peace Treaty conference which settled a long-standing enmity between Pope Alexander III and the Emperor Frederick Barbarossa. This experience inspired Gervasius to study law in Bologna, but he regularly returned to England when the opportunity presented itself.

A few years later, this brilliant young man became adviser to the Archbishop of Reims in France, who was notorious for his cruelty as a heresy convictor. It was during this period, when Gervasius was in his late twenties, that an event occurred which was destined to alter the whole course of his inner life, while leaving his outer activities remarkably unaffected.

We owe the details of the Reims events to the fact that at the end of his long life Gervasius confessed his crime to Ralph of Coggeshall, who preserved his confession. Briefly, whilst in Reims, Gervasius fell in love with a young girl who did not return his affection. This wounded him deeply and roused his passions so strongly that he accused her of being a witch. The Archbishop, who trusted Gervasius without question, decided that the young girl should be burnt at the stake. As Gervasius was the only witness, he was required to be present at the martyrdom of the innocent girl. This became a turning point in his life: as the flames rose, Gervasius experienced her suffering as his suffering, feeling the full weight of his guilt and the radiance of her innocence. He spent the remaining fifty years of his life as a restless wanderer, still frequenting the courts of the princes of Europe, but intent on seeking

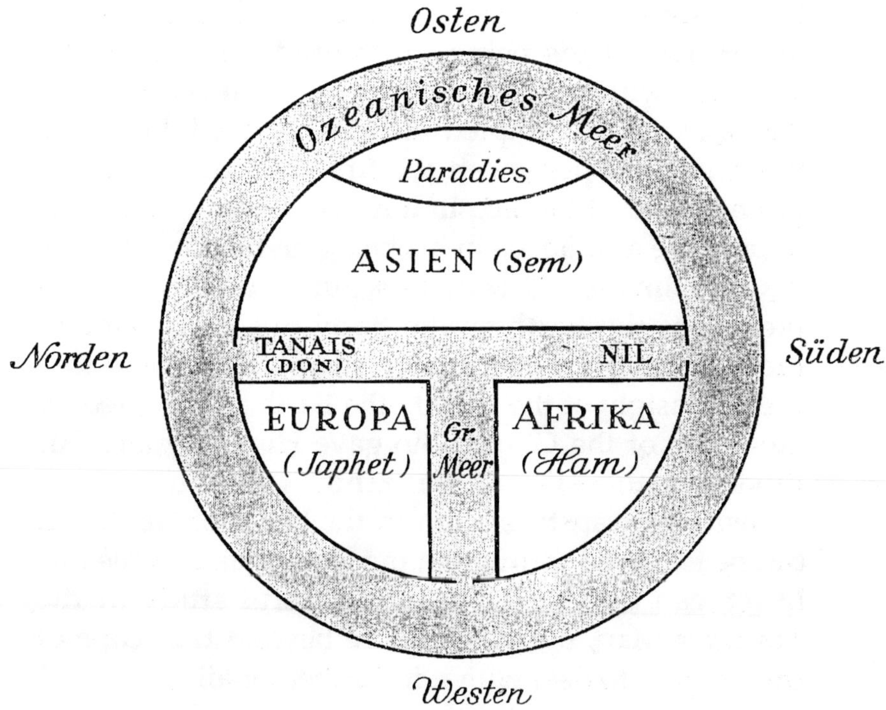
Osten
Ozeanisches Meer
Paradies
ASIEN (Sem)
Norden
TANAIS
(DON)
NIL
Süden
EUROPA
(Japhet)
Gr.
Meer
AFRIKA
(Ham)
Westen

atonement for the terrible deed he had committed. He carried the secret of his guilt all through his life until, shortly before his death, he confessed it. His creation of the Ebstorfer World Map at the end of his life can be seen as the visible fruit of his self-transformation.

This tragic biography illustrates in a remarkable way the path from self-knowledge to world-knowledge. There can be no doubt that it was the lower part of his being, the unredeemed self, the astrality which is the seat of man's passions and desires, which prompted his terrible deed. From the moment he experienced the fire that consumed the girl he loved, it kindled in him the inner fire that was to produce a catharsis in his being on the long road of his pilgrimage. Out of this purified astrality the picture of the Earth as the Body of Christ came to him. Through a deep inner struggle he came to a greater insight of the world: the Earth as ensouled by the Being of the Christ who gave His Body and His Blood for the sake of mankind. Once this fact is known, the transformation in the being of Gervasius can be followed through in the later phases of his life. Much can be learned from a careful study of the Ebstorfer Map, but it would be beyond the scope of this chapter to deal with it in further detail.

The fundamental difference between the maps of Al-Idrisi and of Gervasius will now be obvious: One was produced by the purely utilitarian spirit of outward research, whereasthe other was born out of deep suffering and meditation.

Another individual who viewed the Earth as a

living organism is Leonardo da Vinci. In one of his notebooks dated around 1500 he wrote:

> The Earth has a spirit of growth; its flesh is the soil, its bones the stratifications of the rocks, forming the mountains, its blood the springs of water; and the increase and decrease of blood in the pulses is represented in the Earth by the ebb and flow of the sea.

For Leonardo, everything in nature—even the solid ground—was in a constant state of flux. The source and center of this continuous energy was shrouded in mystery, but the Earth as a living being was for him still a potent reality. What was a reality to Leonardo is now being virtually rejected, as most modern scientific research leads individuals to believe that the Earth is but a speck of dust in the infinitude of the universe.

Thus the Christian conception of the Earth faded away: in several later *T in O* maps we still find the Christ sitting in judgment above the Earth, or the Earth surrounded by a representation of the angelic world; but then this, too, disappears by about the middle of the fourteenth century. Cartographers came to accept the Arabian view of a secular Earth planet devoid of life and divine influence, and the concept of the world as the Body of Christ was completely forgotten.

As we can see, the history of cartography reflects on a small scale what was occurring in the evolution of consciousness in humanity as a whole. Mankind's evolution necessitates that we experience a separation from the spiritual world, for only out of freedom will we be able to realize our true potential. Mankind must now struggle through a conscious path of self-development to regain an integrated picture of himself and the cosmos. Rudolf Steiner repeatedly refers to this path as one which leads from self-knowledge to world knowledge. This path is intimately connected with the Mystery of the Holy Grail, a conscious path of development which leads one to an exhaulted state of love, compassion and responsibility. It is most significant that Rudolf Steiner should refer to the modern initiate as an "Initiate of the Grail."

> We see that the highest imaginable ideal of human evolution results from the "knowledge of the Grail": the spiritualization that man acquires through his own efforts. . . . "wisdom of the external world" becomes inner wisdom of man. Intensified in the inner life, it becomes the seed of love . . . What he there produces in the inmost depths of his soul is finally itself to become the outer world.
>
> *Occult Science, Chapter 6*

It is then the fruit of our own inwardly spiritualized experiences of the Earth which returns to become the transformed Earth itself.

If we now turn to Wolfram von Eschenbach's *Parzival,* we find that a major portion of the training Parzival received from the wise hermit, Treverizent, deals with the Fall of the Earth and its redemption through Christ.

> But his host [Trevrizent] replied, "I shall take away your doubt. If I do not tell you the real truth, you may reproach me for my deception. The Earth was Adam's mother; from the fruits of the Earth Adam lived and nourished himself. And yet the Earth was a virgin. But I have not told you yet who took her virginity from her. Adam was Cain's father. Cain slew Abel for the sake of paltry possessions. When blood then fell upon the pure Earth, her virginity was forfeit, and it was Adam's son who took it from her. Then, for the first time, hatred sprang up among men, and so it has been ever since.
>
> "In all the world there is truly nothing so pure as a maiden innocent of guile. Just think how pure maidens are. God Himself was the Maiden's child. Two men were born of maidens. God Himself took on human countenance like that of the first maiden's child. That was a gracious courtesy from Him Whose nature is so exalted."

By slaying his brother Abel, whose blood flowed into the Earth, Cain robbed the Earth of her virginity. It is not accidental that "Cain" means "spear" in Hebrew, for the first stage of Christ's union with the Earth was accomplished when the spear of Longinus pierced His side. His Blood flowed into the Earth, thereby rejuvenating its substance. This substance, however, cannot thrive without the active participation of mankind. The seed was sown by the

Christ—it is mankind's task to nurture its growth.

The blood of Christ Jesus that flowed in the Earth calls upon our powers of insight and initiative in recognizing the Earth as a living organism. We need not seek the Being of Christ in a supersensible realm outside the Earth. He is active here in the very substance of our physical planet. He can be found not only in the hearts of men and women "who are of good will" but equally potently in the living garment of the Earth. Agriculture, environmental protection, preservation of our natural resources, clean air, and the many related concerns take on an esoteric dimension as we begin to experience the Earth as the Body of Christ.

There lies within the words of the German poet Novalis, a challenge for all of mankind: *Wir sind auf einer Mission: zur Bildung der Erde sind wir berufen.* "We are engaged upon a mission: we are called upon to shape, to fashion the Earth."

Man stands today at a major crossroads. Either he chooses to perpetuate the death-dealing blows of Cain to a wounded Earth, or he chooses to unite himself through the Mysteries of the Holy Grail with the Earth-healing forces of the Christ Who gave His Body and His Blood in sacrifice.

BIBLIOGRAPHY

References to the Holy Grail by Rudolf Steiner (Reprinted by the kind permission of Steven Roboz)

Richard Wagner in the Light of Anthroposophy, 28 March, 1905, Berlin.

Richard Wagner in the Light of Anthroposophy, 19 May, 1905, Berlin.

What Is the Holy Grail?, 23 October, 1905, Berlin.

The Royal Art, 2 January, 1906, Berlin.

Esoteric Cosmology, 8 May, 1906, Paris.

The Grail Mystery in Wagner's Works, 29 July, 1906, Landin.

The Music of *Parsifal,* 16 January, 1907, Kassel.

Theosophy and the Rosicrucians, 6 June, 1907, Munich.

Theosophy and Rosicrucianism, 28 June, 1907, Munich.

Occult Signs and Symbols, 16 September, 1907, Stuttgart.

The Gospel of St. John, 22 November, 1907, Basle.

Occult Science, an Outline, Chapter VI, 1909.

The Festivals and Their Meaning, 11April, 1909, Cologne.

Spiritual Hierarchies, 12 April, 1909, Dusseldorf.

The European Mysteries and Their Initiates, 6 May, 1909, Berlin.

The Gospel of St. John in Its Relation to the Other Three Gospels, 24 June, 1909, Kassel.

The East in the Light of the West, 23 August, 1909.

Esoteric Hour Lecture, 27 August, 1909, Munich.

The Mission of the Folk Souls, 12 June, 1910, Oslo.

Reincarnation and Karma–Their Significance in Modern Culture, 5 March, 1912, Berlin.

Between Death and Rebirth, 7 January, 1913, Berlin.

The Mysteries of the East and of Christianity, 7 February, 1913, Berlin.

The Effects of Spiritual Development, 25 March, 1913, Hague.
The Effects of Spiritual Development, 26 March, 1913, Hague.
Christ and the Spiritual World and the Search for the Holy Grail, 1-2 January, 1914, Leipzig.
From the Akashic Investigations. The Fifth Gospel, 6 January, 1914, Berlin.
From Symptom to Reality in Modern History, 3 November, 1918, Dornach.
The Mysteries of Light, of Space and of the Earth, 13 December, 1919, Dornach.
Man, Hieroglyph of the Universe, 16 May, 1920, Dornach.
Greece in the Period of Its Decline. The Mystery of the Grail, 16 April, 1921, Dornach.
The Materialistic Cognitive Impulse and Its Significance, 17 April, 1921, Dornach.
The Mystery of the Trinity, 23 July, 1922, Dornach.
Supersensible Influences in the History of Mankind, 1 October, 1922, Dornach.
Spiritual Relations in the Configuration of the Human Organism, 22 October, 1922, Dornach.
The Driving Force of Spiritual Powers in World History, 23 March, 1923, Dornach.
World History in the Light of Anthroposophy, 31 December, 1923, Dornach.
Karmic Relationships, Vol VIII, 21 August, 1924, Torquay.
Karmic Relationships, Vol. VIII, 27 August, 1924, London.
Karmic Relationships, Vol. IV, 14 September, 1924, Dornach.
Karmic Relationships, Vol. IV, 16 September, 1924, Dornach.
Karmic Relationships, Vol. IV, 18 September, 1924, Dornach.
Anthroposophical Leading Thoughts, 15 February, 1925, Dornach.

Works by Other Authors

Parzival, Wolfram von Eschenbach, Trans. Mustard and Passage, Vintage Press, 1961.

Medieval Romances, Perceval, Chrétien de Troyes, Modern Library College Editions, 1957.

Parzival, Eileen Hutchins, Temple Lodge Press, 1979.

From Round Table to Grail Castle, Isabel Wyatt, The Lanthorn Press, 1979.

The Grail Legend, Emma Jung and Marie Louise von Franz, Sigo Press, 1971

Zum Raum wird hier die Zeit, Rudolf Meyer, Urachhaus, 1980.

The Grail, Quest for the Eternal, John Matthews, Thomas and Hudson, 1981.

The Ninth Century and the Holy Grail, Walter Johannes Stein, Temple Lodge Press, 1988.

The Death of Merlin, Walter Johannes Stein, Floris Books, 1989.

The Quest of the Holy Grail,, Jessie L. Weston, Frank Cass, 1964.

For Freedom Destined, Mysteries of Man's Evolution in the Mythology of Wagner's Ring Operas and Parsifal, Franz E. Winkler, Waldorf Press, 1974.

The Holy Grail, From the Works of Rudolf Steiner, Compiled by Steven Roboz, Steiner Book Centre, 1984.

Anthroposophy as a Healing Force, L. Francis Edmunds, Fellowship Committee, 1968.

The Golden Age of Chartres: Teachings of a Mystery School and the Eternal Feminine by René M. Querido, Floris Books, 1987.

ABOUT THE AUTHOR

René M. Querido, of Portuguese ancestry, Dutch descent and British nationality, studied mathematics and physics at London University and began his career in Waldorf education at Michael Hall School in England in 1949. He has been active for forty years in the worldwide Waldorf movement, teaching and lecturing in Britain, North America, Germany, Switzerland, France, Mexico, and Japan.

He was formerly the director of Rudolf Steiner College in Fair Oaks, California, and was awarded an honorary doctoral degree for his activities in Waldorf education and for his work on Chartres and on Shakespeare. He has written a number of books and articles published in English, French, Danish, German, Swedish, and Japanese. He is now retired from full-time teaching and is currently General Secretary of the Anthroposophical Society in America. He is the author of *Creativity in Education* and *The Golden Age of Chartres.*